EAT, DRINK & BE MERRY

Kris,
Merry Christmas compliments of your mom-in-law, Mary Lou.
My husband and I are grateful to have made friends with fellow Iowans now calling Texas their home.

Merry Corlin
12-6-2008

EAT, DRINK & BE MERRY

A Memoir By Merry Corbin

iUniverse, Inc.
New York Lincoln Shanghai

EAT, DRINK & BE MERRY

Copyright © 2007 by Merry Corbin

All rights reserved. No part of this book may be used or reproduced by any means, graphic, electronic, or mechanical, including photocopying, recording, taping or by any information storage retrieval system without the written permission of the publisher except in the case of brief quotations embodied in critical articles and reviews.

iUniverse books may be ordered through booksellers or by contacting:

iUniverse
2021 Pine Lake Road, Suite 100
Lincoln, NE 68512
www.iuniverse.com
1-800-Authors (1-800-288-4677)

Because of the dynamic nature of the Internet, any Web addresses or links contained in this book may have changed since publication and may no longer be valid.

The views expressed in this work are solely those of the author and do not necessarily reflect the views of the publisher, and the publisher hereby disclaims any responsibility for them.

ISBN: 978-0-595-45248-4 (pbk)
ISBN: 978-0-595-89560-1 (ebk)

Printed in the United States of America

Contents

FOREWORD vii
GIVE ME A HOUSE 1
THE MAKING OF A SURVIVOR 6
A PIECE OF CAKE 14
BOMBS, BRASSIERES AND BEAUTY OPERATORS 20
HOW DOES YOUR GARDEN GROW 28
GO YE BULLDOGS 39
MARRIAGE MADE IN HAVOC 48
THE BEGETING OF KIDS 54
LOSS OF CLASS 64
HO HO HO 75
A FEW OF MY FAVORITE THINGS 85
JUST FOR THE FUN OF IT 96
THE LAST DANCE 105
AFTERWORD 111

FOREWORD

For several years I've promised or threatened, depending on your point of view, to write a book which sorts out the memorable events of my life. Having taught high school and junior high language arts for twenty-seven years, I've thought a bit about the science and art of writing. Like all literature teachers, I have read my share of books, and indeed, the same book many, many times. I once calculated that I had interpreted Shakespeare's brutal portrayal of the slaying of Julius Caesar more than two hundred times. I would be hard pressed to even estimate the number of student essays I have read and red-marked in my lifetime.

Friends have urged me to write a book. They give various reasons. Some think I have had an unusual and somewhat eventful life. Acquaintances know that I slip a lot of stories into conversations. In fact, I often forget what I was going to say after sidestepping with some details that surely had to be told. Robert Frost said it so eloquently, "But I was going to say, before truth stepped in ..."

The Can-Do factor is always a temptation. On several occasions I have seen people engaged in intriguing activity or admired the results of their efforts. "I can do that" was easy to say, but most of the time I didn't try. Sometimes I tried and failed. A few times that assertive attitude committed me to reach new heights and experience uncharted waters—like writing this book.

I'm actually taking on this project for three extremely special reasons: Carter, Olivia, and Nolan. I would like my GRANDkids to be acquainted with their Grandma Merry and the life style of the Twentieth Century. I intend for them to know what was near and dear to me so that someday they will have valuable family memories and keepsakes to cherish.

But probably even more pressing, is my urge to share what I've learned in life in the hopes of making the little kids' lives easier. I would like to teach the kids to experience every mud puddle they encounter, jumping over it just in time to stay free of the mud yet gleaning every joy and insight each puddle has to offer. If I taught them just that, I might keep on giving forever.

I've known the first line of my story for a long time. What I haven't figured out is how to put the whole thing together—organizational freak that I am. I could use a chronological arrangement with chapters covering the major events of my life. Perhaps a good approach would be chapters detailing lessons learned and advice I want to pass on. I could devote a chapter to each of the major people in my life—Beth and Eve and their families, my parents and grandparents, Aunt Maybelle, Bill and Doris, Beth and Rob, Chris, Fords, and Stewarts, to mention a few. My goal is to finish writing while at least some of those important players are still alive, reassuring them of their importance to me.

I'm thinking, though, that this book will follow a stream of consciousness. I'll let my mind wander carrying thoughts with lots of interjections and bird walks. That imitates my life—doing what comes naturally. Buried somewhere in the middle of my thoughts are values and characteristics pretty easily detected from my experiences. Writing should help me discover myself as well as share the essence of my being with the GRANDkids.

I'm referring to this book as a memoir rather than autobiography. Somewhere I gathered the distinction between the two. Autobiography is a collection of facts written about a person's own life. A memoir details what one recalls, and is not, by its very nature, the absolute truth—just the truth as remembered. I intend to do some research to try to keep my facts straight, but who knows just how rosy the glasses reflect over the years.

Beth asked if my book (which she would prefer I not write) would be fact or fiction. I told her it would be true—my memoirs. She replied that the readers who know me would probably see it as fiction. Possibility. I've also heard that we tend to remember only the good and to forget the bad. I'm not aligned with that generalization either.

That leads to my disclaimer. The names will be of real people. Their names will not be changed and I won't attempt to protect their innocence—or guilt. Rather, I aspire to chronicle my life with the truth of what I recall and the characterization of a few of the significant people I have encountered along the way. Some may disagree with what I say, others will think I should have included something that they deem missing, and still others will think that I should have left something unsaid. I haven't censored my memories and feelings and I don't think it is appropriate to let others do so either. For that reason alone, I am not sharing any of the words written until the book is printed. I don't fancy my memoirs compromised by other people's suggestions.

What I'm going to do with the manuscript when I'm finished is a decision not yet made. My goal is to write. What happens next is always an unknown in life.

So as I wade through major events in my life and elicit the lessons I've learned, I anticipate getting to know myself better. I'm using the opportunity lying ahead to share a little humor and a lot of love for life with friends and family who have the curiosity to read my words.

August 25, 2005, Chapter 1 begins.

for
Nolan, Olivia, and Carter
accompanied by Grandma Merry's hope
for your lives to be rich and wise and
filled with love and laughter

GIVE ME A HOUSE

"Let me live in a house by the side of the road and be a friend to man." The first time I heard these words, I was sitting in the front pew of the United Methodist Church in Lamont in 1966. Pastor Blaylock was preaching the sermon at Grandpa Smith's funeral. Grandma, Bob, Jean, Bill, Doris, Terry, Dian, Sid and I (with Eve in my tummy) more than filled the first pew as we listened to Gaby Stewart play "The Old Rugged Cross" and "In the Garden". Grandpa had a wonderful tenor voice. From the time I was twelve years old, I would play those two hymns on the piano and Grandpa and I would sing. Whenever a really good pianist or another willing singer would visit our home, Grandpa would always get a songfest of hymns going.

I wanted to tell Pastor Blaylock that he should have added a few words to the quote: "And let him be a Democrat." Grandpa had friends who weren't Democrats, but on his list of friends, he probably marked each Democrat with an asterisk. He treasured the letters and pictures taken of him with Ted Kennedy, Senators John Culver and Dick Clark, a local boy made good. Grandpa even arranged for me to dance with Harold Hughes at a grass-roots Democratic shindig long before I was old enough to finish a dance and long before HH was a governor and senator. I was brainwashed with Democratic views during the McCarthy trials, the Stevenson-Kefauver debates, and JFK's win over Nixon. I've often thought Grandpa (and my ears) was spared from ever knowing that Nixon was elected President.

I learned early in life to be a Democrat. As a little girl I sat on a footstool by the radio listening to the election results in hopes that Truman would be elected President. I was only six years old in 1948, but it could have been yesterday, based on the clarity in my mind. It's not a stretch to say I've always been a Democrat and probably goes without saying that there'll be no change.

The minister's words lingered with me because they described Grandpa's life so perfectly. He always kept his forty-acre farm clean and tidy with gates wide open to all his friends. It was customary in the fifties when I was growing up to drop in, though uninvited, to visit friends and relatives whenever the fancy struck. Often by dusk on Sunday, we would have had twenty or thirty people stop by to say hello. And every night—EVERY NIGHT—of my childhood, friends came to play cards. Those people passed years ago, but Ray and Edith Harbit, Skin and Gert Estling, Hank and Dessie Wessels, Ray and Cecile Hall, Dean and Estrid Morris, and Mabel and John Cuthbertson were often around the table.

Since television hadn't entered the picture yet, my entertainment was watching the card playing and waiting for someone to go to the bathroom so that I could play the vacated hand. Most evenings the game was Five Hundred, Canasta, Pinochle or my favorite, Royal Rummy—sometimes called Tripoli. Uncle Bill made a special wooden board for Tripoli in the late forties. I bought it at Grandma's auction after her death in 1981. Bill signed it on a visit to our house in Indianola fifty years after he made it.

And as one might expect, Grandpa had a partner that greatly enhanced his hospitality. Grandma kept her house spiffed up to match the outdoors. But most memorable was the lunch guests must be served before they could leave. Long after I was in bed, the cake, cookies, cold cuts and cheeses came out with strong coffee loaded with caffeine. Grandma always had something home baked. She could stretch her "Whole in the Middle" devil's food cake slathered with white frosting through several groups of company. The dessert was always covered with a heavy plastic bag, too worn to see through, and kept on a refrigerator shelf to maintain its freshness.

While Beth and Eve were growing up on Aspen Lane, I usually had something freshly baked on the counter. Beth's friend Traci remarked years later that when she came to visit she always looked at the counter spot reserved for the home baked goodies. Chances are good that Traci saw *Wacky Cake* sitting on the counter. Beth actually brought the recipe home from her junior high home economics class. Its moistness and rich chocolate flavor reminded me of Grandma's cake.

Wacky Cake

3 cups flour	2 T vinegar
2 cups sugar	3/4 cup cooking oil
6 T cocoa	2 tsp vanilla
2 tsp soda	2 cups cold water
1 tsp salt	

Make and bake the cake in a 9 x 13 ungreased pan. Sift dry ingredients into pan. Add liquids into cake pan and stir well. Bake at 350 for 35 minutes or until toothpick comes out clean.

*   *   *

The best advice I ever got from anyone came from Grandma Smith. She always said, "When in doubt, don't." Those are valuable words that I have said to myself hundreds of times and probably passed on to Sid and the girls that many times, as well. If an action or a statement is questioned before it occurs, it is a forewarning not to proceed. Good advice. I wish I would have **always** heeded her reminder, but I didn't, even though it rests permanently on my conscience and helps keep me on the right path most of the time.

"Let me live in a house by the side of the road and be a friend to man." The second time I heard these words, the setting was my classroom. As a language arts teacher, I had a variety of things to teach—grammar, composition, speech, and literature. Within the literature, I preferred poetry. Routinely I asked students to do research outside of the classroom to find a favorite poem to analyze and share with me. One of my students at Marion, Karen Luko, submitted "The House by the Side of the Road" written by Sam Walter Foss. I was delighted to finally receive the complete poem and discover its author.

That familiar line reappeared twenty-five years later. It flowed out of my mind and landed on a blank sheet of paper. I was attending a Stephen Covey seminar; we were asked to develop a goal statement by the end of the week's soul searching. Not to my surprise, mine was a poem that said:

*Give me a house beside the Road
and let me be a Friend,
Give me a house beside the Lake
and let me reflect on the Water,
Give me a house beside the Woods
and let me commune with Nature,
Give me a house beside the Garden
and let me share beauty with Flowers.*

I was beginning to think about retiring when I wrote the poem. Ideals that were dear to me all my life would remain the theme for retirement. As I recall stories I aspire to tell, my relationship with friends and my attentiveness to homes poke in everywhere.

"One could do worse than be a swinger of birches." How often I have quoted Robert Frost's *Swinging on Birches* and filled in the blank to suit my needs. One could do worse than living at the side of the road and being a friend. The heartfelt phrase could eulogize my life as well as it spoke for Grandpa Smith years ago. "Let me live in a house by the side of the road and be a friend to man."

THE MAKING OF A SURVIVOR

I grew up. Sometimes that was all I wanted to say. My childhood was confusing. I still don't know whether to contend that it was normal, as I usually did. Or should I say no one else could understand it, as I sometimes professed. But two things are certain, I always say that I had a good childhood and I rarely burden my friends with the sordid details unless pushed to do so. I have had lots of friends and pretty close acquaintances that do not know me as the survivor following my family's passing.

The home I remember was three miles south and two miles west of Lamont on a typical Iowa farm until the day my life drastically changed when I was five years old. I have challenged myself to remember those first five years. The snippets of memory that remain are from a four or five-year-old's observation. I have very few pictures from that time and no pictures of the things I remember. Most of my memories could not have been told to me because people who survived were not involved in the recollections that I cherish. Memories are priceless and I have sole possession.

Over the years I have come to know that the things I remember were things that were VERY important to me. Some of them are mundane things, but I share them because they reveal who I am.

Ours was a busy household. My mom had four children and the oldest was six when she died. The story is told that my parents celebrated the first birthday of each child by starting another. Probably some truth exists in that statement since we were each about twenty-one months younger that our older sibling.

Many of my memories of our house involve neatness—or lack of. I particularly remember the summer day when my mother hosted the Lutheran Ladies Aid meeting at our house. I was so proud because the front porch floor got a fresh coat of golden brown paint, and the guests entered through the front instead of the side door, which led to the farm yards and easy parking for familiar guests.

My bedroom was on the second floor with my brothers. I don't remember much besides two beds and the stairway, probably because not much else was there. The upstairs was above only a small portion of the first-floor. I do remember being awakened in the night to take my older brother down the stairs to the outside toilet. He was afraid of the dark and I wasn't. Another night the upstairs seemed less than pleasant when one of my brothers was sick. My dad awakened the Jenks family across the road to borrow aspirin from them. I have always wondered why anyone could be out of aspirin. Perhaps that explains my careful planning to avoid running out of supplies.

The Jenks family had two girls who were all grown up in my eyes. They were probably teenagers at the time. One day they asked me to go to Forestville Beach with them. I lay on the blanket sunning with them in awe of their painted fingernails. I don't remember their names but I can still picture that bright red paint on their beautiful fingernails. I could count on one hand the number of times my nails have not been painted in the last twenty-five years.

At that same Ladies Aid meeting, I remember being complimented on my pretty dress. Grandma Otterbeck had made it for me out of flour sacks. I was delighted to go to my room when directed to display the other beautiful dress she had sewn for me. My dresses hung on a hook on the back of the bedroom door. The house had no closets that I know of. We probably didn't have much to hang up in those days.

Grandma O. was handy with the sewing machine. She made drapes and dresser skirts, and she reupholstered chairs. I would like to think that I inherited some of her ingenious and frugal decorating skills. I certainly have done my share of decorating in my homes and especially for Beth and Eve. Even though I detest sewing, my portable Sears sewing machine purchased in the early seventies has logged more miles than most cars. I've dragged it along to the girls' houses countless times to make window treatments, sew up a seam or make a simple slip cover. Sid and the girls learned early on to clear the nest when the sewing machine appears because they're pretty certain combat will erupt between the machine and me.

Good old-fashioned cooking was one of Grandma O's legacies. For years I made mashed potatoes just like she did—whipped, with lots of cream and a big dollop of butter. The potatoes were raised in her garden; the cream was separated from the milk Grandpa brought in from the barn; the butter was churned from the extra cream. I never thought those heavenly mashed potatoes could be surpassed, but tastes change and even cooking gets updates. I'm including the mashed potato recipe I prefer today.

Mashed Potatoes

32 oz can chicken broth with sodium	2 T soft butter
6 large red potatoes, unpeeled, halved	1/2 tsp pepper
2 chopped garlic cloves	1/4 cup reserved broth
1/2 cup cream	3 slices cooked bacon, crumbled

Boil scrubbed potatoes and garlic in broth. Drain, reserving broth. Mash and whip potatoes using cream, butter, pepper, and reserved broth. Add more broth or cream if needed for desired consistency. Stir in bacon and 1/4 cup fresh chopped chives.

* * *

The stores in Lamont and all little farm communities used to be open on Saturday night. It was a big deal for farm families to go to town to culminate the long work week. I don't actually remember going to town but I do remember almost NOT going. We were eating "supper", as the evening meal used to be called. Dinner was the big meal served at noon because the farmers still had a half-day of work left. Scalloped corn was one of the dishes being served that evening and neither Terry nor I wanted to eat it. My dad said we had to eat it or we couldn't go to town. We both gagged it down. Terry probably still doesn't like scalloped corn but it has become one of the traditional vegetables served at our family holiday meals.

I'm not very fond of raisins, and for good reason. I had really long dark blonde hair that I hated to have brushed. It was full of natural curl and snarls. The long curls were cut off when I was six and still occupy a box stored in the cedar chest. I preferred to avoid the pain from snarl removal by standing in front of the mirror in my parents' bedroom to brush my hair myself. When my mom took the brush into her hands, I was rewarded with raisins—my favorite snack—if I stood still and didn't complain. One day, I decided to explore behind the cloth curtain that hid the pantry from the kitchen. I found the raisins and ate them until I became sick.

Our kitchen table was visible as we came down the stairs each morning. I particularly remember getting up early on Easter Sunday and racing down in anticipation of the loot from the Easter Bunny. I don't remember what the Easter Bunny left that day, but I do remember the kitchen table was ready for breakfast. Two cereal boxes sat on the table; I didn't think that looked very tidy. I never allowed cereal boxes on the table at my house. I also always served the milk in a pitcher—no cartons on the table either. I still have the brown stoneware pitcher that held the cream Mom doled out at the farm.

I used to watch Mom eat ice cream and would try to eat it just like she did, but I lacked her patience. Her favorite flavor was chocolate. She would carve a spoonful out of her bowl, put the whole thing into her mouth, and carefully pull the spoon back out revealing a dome shaped, but smooth, top. After eyeing the remains, she would insert the spoon for a second bite. This time as she pulled it out ever so slowly, the top was level but still very smooth. The third bite was taken and the empty spoon was revealed only to start the savoring process all over again by filling up the spoon.

My mom loved Mars candy bars packaged in a brown and green wrapper. They had soft centers with whole almonds lined up in a single row on top and were finally dipped in milk chocolate. I used to buy them once in awhile to remember Mom, even though they were not my favorite. I haven't noticed them in the stores for the last several years.

The dining room on the farm was in the center of the house between the kitchen and the living room. That's where guests landed when they came in from the front porch. A large mahogany table, circa 1930, and matching buffet graced the room. I don't ever remember eating at that table. I remember climbing on it and using a chair to navigate from there to the top of the buffet. As an adult I figured out why there were never any adornments on either piece of furniture. Eve bought a very similar antique set in Davenport shortly after she and Dave were married. Hers has two additional pieces to complete the set. I think of my family's dining room every time I see Eve's.

My parents' bedroom was off the dining room. It boasted the mirrored dresser that was the scene of the hair brushing. The other memory I have is my mom lying on the bed nursing my youngest brother, Willis. She would be disgusted with him for biting her. He was eleven months old when he died. I don't know if he was weaned by then or not but I imagine she enjoyed that short rest she got with his feeding time. My children were bottle-fed.

I have a bracelet on the arm of a favorite white bear in our den. The bear is wearing my bracelet made from a continuous strand of gold that spells out "Merry". It was a gift from my parents' outing to the Cattle Congress in Waterloo. I slept lightly that night so I would be sure to hear them come home to fulfill their promise of bringing me something. Clara Flaucher was our baby sitter. She was a capable Lamont fixture who used her mothering and housekeeping skills to help many families in the area.

Last year when Beth (Mary Beth Ford) and Rob Hampel visited, she remarked that she had a bracelet just like mine. Neither of us knows for sure, but we would like to think that our parents went together to the Cattle Congress that day. Doc and Fran were good friends of my parents.

One of the stories from my childhood that Doc told me was very revealing of the fun my parents had with Fords. Doc said he would call our house and always say, "Well, Yula, you're pregnant again." He knew he could get her goat since the neighbors on the party line were probably listening. The phone was a big monster made of oak that hung on the wall. Lillian Ivory was the phone operator in town. One turn of the handle would reach her. We told her to whom we wanted to speak and she would plug into a couple of circuits and crank out the ring. A long and two shorts reached our house. I envision every one else running to pick up the phone to listen as the ringer sounded in all the homes on the party line.

Another time I remember getting up in the middle of the night when I heard a commotion down stairs. A strange noise was coming from my dad's car. He opened the trunk to discover a cat screaming its head off. He had gone to town alone that evening and evidently was the butt of a joke from one of his friends who imagined the explanations Roger would have to make to my mother that night when he got home.

Doors in cars or houses didn't get locked at that time and keys were left in cars. It wasn't an issue except for the occasional practical joke. Apparently no one needed to be kept out. Our screen doors had a drop-in hook high on the inside of the door to keep the little kids in.

One special night I got to go to a basketball game at Lamont High School from which both of my parents had graduated. It was my turn to go with Dad while everyone else stayed home. I wore a gold jumper with black trim on the pocket—probably the handy work of Grandma Otterbeck again. My mom dressed me in a white blouse under the jumper and placed a barrette to hold back my long hair. Comments were pretty special as my dad showed me off to everyone. He told me the black trim on my pocket was an L that stood for Lamont, just like the cheerleaders wore. He was covering up one side of the trim to display the L.

I remember Donna Whitney staying at our house and helping Mom with the household duties. Today she would be called a nanny or a maid. Housework was a common career for women at that time. It must have been a real chore for a mother of four without hot water, to say nothing of a spigot for it to come out of. The washing machine with the wringer attached was moved each summer from the back room to the outside of the house to be closer to the clothes line.

Most of all, I remember how Donna would get dressed up to go out in the evening, but not without my dad teasing her. The last thing before she left, I would watch her carefully put on her dark red lipstick. If for some reason I remained awake when she came home, I would watch her go to the same mirror to carefully remove her lipstick. I started wearing make up when I was a teenager and still don't like to be caught without it. I always confessed that any beauty I had was in a bottle since I had nothing natural going for me.

My last childhood memory of my family and home was Christmas, four days before they died. Pictures remain of the toys Santa left and of Grandpa and Grandma Smith and Bill and Doris, who weren't yet married. One memory I have of that night is not pictured. I can still see Santa coming through the kitchen door carrying a rope. Terry, Larry and I were given the rope and told to hold on tight so that the reindeer didn't get away. We tugged as hard as we could; the reindeer would give an occasional jerk. Santa distributed his toys and grabbed the rope on his way out. Later I was told that Bill was playing Santa, and the rope was tied to a tree where Dad pulled on it enough to excite Terry, Larry and me on the other end.

As I think back to my memories, I happily recall things from the early years that have remained important to me for life. Fortunately, I can't miss what I didn't know I had. Such is the nature of life. Except, I always wanted to call someone Mom and I always wished for parents to call me their daughter. But I survived, mainly because I had daughters and they called me Mom. Grandma, a role my mother never got to enjoy, is just one more of those special perks in life.

A PIECE OF CAKE

I took a writing class in the mid-eighties, along with hundreds of other teachers throughout Iowa, called the Iowa Writing Project. We went to class all day for at least a couple of weeks and we wrote and wrote. Lots of teachers gained confidence in their writing abilities during the course. We had, after all, been a generation too early for formal writing instruction like we know it today. I wrote "A Piece of Cake" to be published in our class anthology at the end of the course. I'm sharing it here.

The old bleached pine cupboard stood alone by the frosted window at the end of the primitive kitchen. The battered, enameled work shelf was often pulled out and cluttered with mixing bowls, empty jars, cold left-over potatoes to be fried for breakfast or supper, and spilled flour clinging to everything. Behind the lower left door was the box of raisins Mother saved for a treat when I kept my long curly hair brushed and snarl-free, no easy task for a five-year old. But the biggest treat of all was to have the shelf wiped clean and slid back into place, adorned only with the freshly baked dessert for our supper.

This particular cold December day the cupboard was the way I liked to see it. Sitting neatly on it was the spice cake Mom had tediously mixed and baked a short time earlier. The familiar white enameled cake pan had its share of nicks and knife scrapes producing scattered black spots on the handles of each end. My favorite white icing must have been hurriedly put on a warm cake that time because it was especially glazed looking.

As Mom carried my littlest brother and Larry toddled along with me, I glanced at that cake sitting temptingly on the cupboard as we hurried to join Dad in the new Plymouth. He was anxious to get to the locker to pick up our freshly butchered meat so that he wouldn't be late getting back for chores. I was anxious to get home for our family supper that I knew would culminate with that cake.

We didn't have cake for supper that night. There were no more suppers. There was no longer a family. The memory of the cake cooling on the often-used cupboard is still vivid in my mind nearly forty years later. But now it has become a symbol, a symbol of a mother's love and caring that I had for comfort the rest of my life.

Sixty years have passed since "the accident" as it came to be known and twenty years since I wrote "A Piece of Cake". I have never written the rest of the story of that day, but I remember it vividly.

My recollection begins with being removed from the backseat of the car sitting with its nose pointed down resting diagonally in the ditch on the right hand side of the road. I don't remember a crash. I don't remember a gravel truck. I don't remember seeing anyone else in the car. Nor do I recall any injuries or pain. I was carried to a man's waiting lap in the back seat of a car at the side of the road. Larry and Willis were there, too, and being held in the arms of men that I didn't know. The little boys were both whimpering and I assured them more than once that we would all be fine and that they shouldn't cry.

I remember pointing out Aunt Maybelle's farm on Highway 3 as we hurried to the Oelwein hospital in what I learned later was Dr. Anderson's car. I was carried up some wide, speckled gray and black terrazzo steps and taken into a huge room filled with chrome lights and medical equipment like you would expect in an operating room.

The next thing I remember, I was in a large, dim room with my brothers, Larry and Willis. We were separated by rolling, wooden screens with gathered white fabric stretched on the frames. I couldn't see the boys but I recognized their cry. I tried to quiet them. I realized years later that they died in that room while I slipped into unconsciousness. I was no longer trying to comfort them, but I was there. They didn't die alone.

My next remembrance was of waking up in a hospital room. Rows of people were facing my bed. I recall a dozen or more men and women, all wearing winter coats, looking at me. The only person I specifically remember seeing was my Aunt Helen, my mom's older sister. In thinking about this scene over the years, I realize that by this time I was the only one who had survived the accident. I think these people had come to visit me sometime during the five days of preparation for the funeral, if not on that day itself. Newspaper clippings confirm that my parents were dead at the scene and that Willis lived eleven hours and Larry lived twenty-four hours.

My first recollection of being spoiled occurred in the hospital room. My bed allowed me to see out a window and into the room across the hall. From my command post, I could get most anything I wanted. I particularly had Doctor Anderson under control. A little red clock that was actually a bank sat on the bed-stand; I coerced him into putting some coins in it everyday he visited me. Although I don't remember suffering, I've been told that I had a broken leg, a broken pelvis, severe internal bleeding and a fish hook lodged above one eye. I was unconscious for a time, but just how long no one seemed to recall after awhile. Penicillin was a new phenomenon in 1947 following World War II. I was given huge doses which probably saved my life but which probably were not the best thing for me. I still avoid penicillin because of an allergic reaction. I never had any childhood diseases like mumps, measles, or chicken pox that I might have been having at that age.

I asked about my family, particularly my mother, when I was still in the hospital. I was always told that she was sick, too, and in another room at the hospital. One time I said I wanted to go to her room; the nurse told me she was in a different hospital.

Later, when I was in a hospital bed in the dining room at Grandpa and Grandma Smith's apartment above the shop, I found out the truth. The young minister from the Lutheran church in Lamont came and told me the story of a little lamb that had lost her Mom. The sun was shining through the window in the kitchen as I watched him walk away after completing what must have been a difficult task for him. I understood what he had told me, but I reacted with little or no remorse making, I suspect, his job much easier.

I have always thought that "the accident" was much harder on other people than it was on me. I was, after all, so young that I didn't remember much of life as it was with my parents. Terry, at six, attended the funeral and certainly had more years to remember following his dad around the farm. He was not in the accident since his second grade classroom was in session that day. It was December 29 and kids were going to school to make up for snow days that had already been missed the winter of '47.

All four of my grandparents witnessed not only their child and spouse die but also two grandchildren. In my worst nightmare, I can't imagine losing just one of those family members at such a young age—or at any age during my lifetime. My aunts and uncles suffered immensely from the loss of their siblings and have always remained dear to me while doing all they could to fill in the gap. Uncle Bill and Aunt Doris were close because they lived and worked nearby or visited his parents, Grandpa and Grandma Smith, often.

Aunt Maybelle was willing for me to stay with her frequently for a few days while I was growing up. She was more than helpful in planning my wedding and my installation as Worthy Advisor of Rainbow Girls. She is still a remarkable and dear Aunt at 92 years of age. She was a PEO member for years in Strawberry Point and Florida. Because of her, I was anxious to join PEO when invited in Indianola.

Aunt Jean, my dad's sister, was Grandpa and Grandma's only daughter. I played with her oldest children, Karen and Lynne, and had many birthday and Christmas celebrations to cherish with both of them.

I still have the lists of flowers, visitors, sympathy cards, and newspaper clippings from those dark days. The communities of Lamont and Strawberry Point, where my parents had lived and their families and friends still resided, were very responsive and grief stricken. Once in awhile I hear of a family of four or more succumbing to death in a car accident. It often makes CNN News. We didn't have television then but the impact was felt pretty widely and locals certainly remembered it.

For decades, I was always introduced as Roger and Yula's daughter. The affirmative response from everyone indicated that they knew what that meant. The visits to the cemetery every Memorial Day kept the reminders going as well. The photo album of my growing-up-years displays several pictures of the Campton Cemetery at Lamont with graves opulently decorated.

Even though we have lived many miles away, I have only failed twice in nearly sixty years to visit the cemetery Memorial weekend. And both of those times, Bill and Doris and my cousin Jacquie took flowers to the cemetery for me.

Doc and Fran Ford took their Christmas evergreen wreath from their front door to the cemetery on December 29 for many, many years. On the few occasions that I still go by the cemetery in the winter, I am reminded that Doc and Fran are gone also. I am pleased to attend to their graves for Beth when I'm near Lamont and she isn't.

Fran was the friendliest role model a young girl could hope to have. She knew no strangers, accepted all weirdoes and liked every living soul she ever encountered. She included us for thanksgiving dinner until her cooking days were over. We still get out her leftovers—the *Glazed Pecan* recipe.

Glazed Pecans

1/2 cup brown sugar	1/8 tsp cloves
1/2 tsp salt	1/8 tsp nutmeg
1/2 tsp cinnamon	1 1/2 T water
1/2 tsp allspice	1 lb pecans

In medium glass bowl, mix all ingredients except pecans and microwave for 1 1/2 minutes. Stir in pecans. Heat 5 minutes on high, stirring every minute. Spread on waxed paper to dry. Break apart and store in tightly covered jar.

*   *   *

Doc was a wonderful source of stories about my family and often expressed what good friends he and my father were. He told me that he was called at his office to go to the scene of the accident but that he couldn't when learning that his good friend was involved. For sure Dad and Doc are yuking it up in heaven. Doc promised me that.

The fact that Doctor Anderson attended to me was probably very critical in how the second stage of my life would take shape. When it was time for me to be dismissed from the hospital, Doctor Anderson called Grandpa Smith and told him to pick me up from the hospital. He responded that Grandpa and Grandma Otterbeck were supposed to do that. I was told later that it was first agreed that Terry would stay with Smiths and I would go with Otterbecks. I'm guessing the decision to split us up was for the sake of fairness and to help each side of the family get past the tragedy. Later I also learned that Uncle George wanted Terry because He didn't have a son, but he already had two daughters. However, Doctor Anderson stood his ground and we both went to live with Grandpa and Grandma Smith.

BOMBS, BRASSIERES AND BEAUTY OPERATORS

It was a good year, 1942, the year of my birth. OK, so everyone likes to think her birth year was a good year. Probably historians wouldn't give 1942 that distinction. I've learned some things to help put my generation in perspective and give the GRANDkids my personal look at history.

I was a war baby. World War II was in full force and dominated most of the news to say nothing of the life style of almost everyone. The world headlines that year proclaimed *BRITISH RAID GERMAN CITIES; JAPANESE MOVE INTO PHILIPPINES; U.S. BOMBS FRANCE, ITALY AND TOKYO.*

On state side in 1942, headlines read *ATOMIC FISSION ACHIEVED; GASOLINE RATIONING; 488 SHIPS BUIILT IN ONE YEAR; U.S. SENDS 100,000 JAPANESE-AMERICANS TO CAMPS;*

ROOSEVELT (President Franklin D.) ASKS CONGRESS FOR 53 BILLION FOR WAR EFFORT; and *DRAFT AGE LOWERED TO 18.*

From the headlines, the war story is obvious. It was only the year before my birth that Japan bombed the United States at Pearl Harbor and a couple of years later that the United States retaliated with the bombing of Iwo Jima.

I wasn't touched by the war directly, but my mom's brother, Bill Otterbeck, was in the Navy and served on a ship harbored in Japan. My dad's brother, Bill Smith, was in the navy when the war ended and was stationed near Washington DC where he had office duties. The story was that my dad would have gone to war except that he was having children and was a farmer—both honorable professions aiding in the war.

The economics of the year were obviously driven by the war. The average income was $1885. A new Ford, Lincoln, Mercury or Plymouth could be purchased for $920. Or you could buy a new house for $3,775. A loaf of bread was 9 cents, a gallon of milk was 60 cents and a gallon of gas was 15 cents. Roughly sixty year later, the average household income is $46,326. In Iowa, the average house costs $106,500 and the average price of a car is $27,950. Today I pay $1.89 for a loaf of bread, $3.00 for a gallon of milk, and a gallon of gas has hit $3.00. A quick round of math reveals that the average income went up 2357% and loaf of bread increased 2000%. That might be progress—but certainly not with a capital P.

Life expectancy in 1942 was 62.9 years. I'm happy I made it past that. I guess this is the bonus time of my life. The life expectancy of women born today is 81. Longevity is in my family. I was fortunate to have all four of my grandparents still living to attend my wedding. Grandma O died at 80 and Grandpa O at 91. Grandma Smith lived to be 83. We all marvel at Aunt Maybelle who is 92 at this time and still very active in mind and body. All four of my grandparents had heart attacks or strokes that finally took their lives. However, Grandpa Smith died of lung cancer even though he smoked cigars and a pipe, not cigarettes.

Genealogists have chronicled my dad's heritage. Grandpa Martin Smith came from a family of eleven reared on Iowa farms in Delaware County. They were of European descent with enough Irish from Margaret Hagerty to justify green beer on St Patrick's Day. Grandma Hazel Smith was a Keiser and her mother was from the Traver family. Both families were prosperous farmers around Manchester, Iowa, where they are buried. Grandma's mother Alice died when giving birth to a son. Her father Will, who twice lost a wife to childbirth, married her Aunt Sophia, sister to his first wife Alice. Those ancestors were European, but primarily British.

Grandpa Christian Otterbeck was born in Germany. His family immigrated to Iowa when he was a young boy. His mother was pregnant and delivered twins three months after arriving in the states. She cared for her other three children in the hold of the cargo ship. My cousins and I who remember the physical appearance of our Great Aunts and Uncles think there may have been some Black mixed with the Caucasian in the generations before my Otterbeck ancestors set sail from Europe. Grandma Agusta (Eder) Otterbeck, like Grandpa, was a German Lutheran raised on farms in Clayton County, Iowa. We female descendants have goose-bump skin on our legs which my kids call Otterbeck bumps. We've never known whether to attribute the bumps to Grandpa or Grandma. For sure, Grandma O contributed the big boob gene. And the story that always surfaces when we talk about the Eder side is that Grandma had a cousin named Peter—Peter Eder.

So I claim to be mostly German. I found it interesting that several people in Malta guessed that Sid and I were German. They were sure we weren't British, like most of the island's visitors. When we revealed our United States citizenship, the Maltese were shocked that we would come from such a large, wonderful country to stay on their little island. They would do anything to get to the States since the number of emigrations granted was quite limited. The Maltese perspective was refreshing. Just the year before, we were in London when the Iraq war broke out. Protest signs were abundant denouncing the United States.

How I got to a discussion of Malta and England when blubbering about 1942, I'm not quite sure. But let's leave that bird walk and go back to the good year.

Aunt Maybelle named me. A few days after my birth, she wrote a letter to my Mom in the hospital and said, "Why don't you name her something pretty like Merry Dee?" The letter has been saved all these years. Many times I have had to explain that I was not born on Christmas. The name is a result of my older brother named Terry Lee. The obvious follow up to the conversation is, "What about your younger siblings—Berry, Jerry, Kerry?" No, they were Larry and Willis.

November 21, 1942, was a Saturday. That's always been my favorite day of the week. I loved tending to the house and garden on a day off from work. I especially liked Saturday night out for dinner and dancing or bridge or hanging out with friends. Saturdays in the fall always meant a Hawkeye Football game since we had season tickets for twenty years. A friend, Vic Klopfenstein, and Wayne Jackson, a teacher at Marion, share my birthday.

Many Americans still famous today were also born in 1942. Musicians Barbara Streisand, Wayne Newton, Paul Simon, Paul McCartney, Aretha Franklin, and Tammy Wynette, boxer Muhammad Ali, quarterback Roger Staubach, and designer Calvin Klein are all my age.

Some of the newly advertised discoveries of the year were Dupont's cellophane wrap, Shinola shoe polish, Kleenex tissues in a box, Lifesavers and LifeBoy Soap.

During my lifetime, monumental changes have occurred, probably the greatest of which was television. It brought the world together. We learned what others were eating, wearing, viewing, and visiting. "Keeping up with the Joneses" took on new dimensions. The news, weather and sports were easily obtained as was fame and fortune.

First TV sets and first TV shows are memorable events of my generation. Our first television was housed in a limed oak cabinet and had a 21-inch screen. I was about twelve years old when we got it. We had three channels—CBS, ABC and NBC. We were lucky to be able to see all three quite well with the antennae on top of the roof. I don't remember the first show we watched but our early TV viewing included *I Love Lucy*, and Edward R. Murrow on the news. Murrow was a favorite carried over from radio.

TV went off the air at night after the ten o'clock news. The last thing we heard was "The Star Spangled Banner" and the last thing we saw was the test pattern. Sometimes, perhaps in reflection of what had just ended or for lack of spirit to move, I stared at the test pattern before going to bed. Television was not on the air on Sunday mornings since most people were in church at that time.

Black and white 12-inch television screens were born and grew up to colored 32-inch screens. Now we have plasma, LCD, High Definition with huge screens, and a whole bunch of other upgrades I don't even understand. We've gone from Video to Digital Video Recordings and TIVO to watch whatever we want at a more convenient time. Sid and I watched very little television until our retirement years. Actually we would not have had a television when we got married except it was part of a large console that housed the stereo system which played our 33 and 45-rpm vinyl records.

Beth and Eve were in high school when "the new" mainframe computers programmed with strange languages were beginning to be replaced with the PC. Now, of course, they are mobile and wireless and every home has a couple and every kid learns on them at school. Sid used the DIBOL computer language to develop programs for inventory, accounts payable, accounts receivable and point of sale at Smulekoff's in the mid eighties. As system analyst, his retirement meant the store had to also retire the old mainframe that he helped establish and kept running for fifteen years.

In the late eighties I took my first PC course with other teachers when computers were added to our classrooms. Later, a large part of my administrative job at Indianola was managing technology. We established a wireless LAN to connect all the buildings and outfitted every classroom with a computer and established at least one lab in each elementary building and eight labs at the middle school and high school. We offered countless staff development courses as we purchased software for use in the classroom and developed a district e-mail system and web page.

A truckload of other far-reaching inventions was born after I was. The dishwasher, sink disposal, microwave oven, automatic washing machine, food freezer, clothes dryer, and electric vacuum sweeper were a few of the conveniences that came along to make housekeeping easier. Grandpa and Grandma built a new house when I was six. An automatic dishwasher, sink disposal, food freezer, forced-air furnace, automatic washing machine, and a double garage were pretty unusual for small town Iowa at that time. Sid's family didn't have indoor plumbing or electricity. He walked to a one-room country schoolhouse with a wood-burning stove that he stoked when his turn came around. When we talked about childhoods, our girls often questioned if we grew up in the same generation. We did.

The health scene has changed dramatically. We did not have health insurance until the kids were well into grade school. The five-day hospital bill for their births was $300 including the doctor bill. Penicillin, birth control pills, and vaccinations for polio were discoveries that were welcomed. Contact lenses saved a lot of vanities. Diagnostic tools like the MRI, CAT scanner and laser surgery saved lots of lives. Newly discovered diseases and health problems like AIDS, West Nile Disease and Autism became huge dreaded maladies desperately needing cures.

When I was a little kid we would get these horrendous bacterial infections called boils. I hardly hear of them anymore. They had a core that had to come out before the sore would heal. Sometimes, they worked themselves out from under the skin and other times the doctor had to lance them. They were highly contagious and they left nasty scars. Gross. But the most painful thing I ever had was a spinal tap—two in one day—when I was diagnosed with spinal meningitis following a pretty bad case of the Asian Flu about 1956.

Over time, lots of the changes were just in terminology. Beth and Eve still cringe when I talk about my beauty operator and spray net instead of my hair designer and hair spray. Brassiere has been shortened to bra. Petting was not allowed but now no one even knows what it was.

We all managed just fine for years without credit cards, ball point pens, laser beams, pantyhose, air conditioning, king and queen-sized beds, FM radio (not to mention satellite radio), water beds, tape decks, CDs, day care centers, group therapy, condominiums, time shares, space travel, cell phones, power lawn mowers, video games, fast food, yogurt, instant coffee, lattes, pizza, McDonalds and Wal-Mart. I must admit, though, that I'm glad all these inventions came along to make life interesting, if not easier.

One of the few" upgrades" we haven't taken advantage of is a queen or king-sized bed. We chose a beautiful walnut bedroom set when we got married. It, like most beds at that time, was a standard double bed. We are fond of the furniture, particularly the headboard and footboard, so we have continued to sleep in the little bed. I don't know anyone else who hasn't upgraded. In fact, it is becoming difficult to buy bedding for a double bed since most purchasers want the larger sizes. We are already antiques and the bed will soon be too.

On the morality side, almost all families had a mom and a dad. Men and women did not live together until they were married and hopefully all children followed the marriage date by at least nine months. Gay and lesbian rights weren't at issue because no one had come out of the closet. And mothers stayed at home and only a handful of them had college degrees. D-i-v-o-r-c-e was barely whispered and rarely occurred in the fifties.

We listened to big band music like Tommy Dorsey and Benny Goodman on records, AM radio with favorite comedy shows like *Amos and Andy*, and Nashville stations playing country music in the middle of the night. Then we upgraded to 8-track tapes and then to cassettes to listen to our favorite artists. No sooner did we have those collections in place, than along came the CD and we had to upgrade again. I always had the favorite songs of Elvis, no matter what system was current. The new players all had FM radio for more music and better listening. Now I've gotten in step with XM radio and favorite tunes are downloaded to an MP3 player. I'm probably already out of date again with technology, but blissfully, I don't know that.

I am at the top end of the baby boomers and Beth is at the bottom end. I always found it interesting that mother and daughter could have the same classification. We Baby Boomers get the blame and credit for many monumental changes. I suppose most people think they lived in the era of big changes, but what other era can claim the dawn of e-mail.

And so life began for me in 1942 and things started happening "big time" right after WW II. And now sixty-five years later, so many things are gone and forgotten that I saw come in and prosper. It's been a long time since I've seen an elevator operator, a pair of nylons, a pneumatic tube carrying money to a central cash register in JC Penney's, a pool hall, rabbit ears for television reception, a tape player, a hi-fi player, bobby pins, spats, linoleum, DDT, plastic records and computer punch cards.

HOW DOES YOUR GARDEN GROW

I grew up in Lamont along with the corn and the cows. Growing things—that's what held people together. Whether you were growing tomatoes in the garden, beans in the field, hay in the pasture, hogs in the barnyard, or kids in the house, you were growing something.

Little by little in the sixties, the town stopped growing as the high school closed and the three grocery stores dwindled to one and eventually to none. All four of the farm implement dealers closed up shop. Thompson Hardware, Smith Plumbing and Heating, Lorenzen's General Store, Colton's Shoe Store, Homewood Café, Smitty's DX and Tudor's Sinclair all met their demise. Dozark's and Miller's taverns didn't even last. The bank and post office remained after Doc Stewart ended his veterinarian practice and Doc Ford stopped seeing patients. When Lamont was booming in the fifties, there were over 700 people living in town. Grandpa always said that Lamont paid the highest sales tax per capita in Iowa during that time.

Today, there is not much happening on the main street and the population is less than half of what it once was. But somehow, lots of the old buildings remain, and some have been kept in pretty good repair. However, Grandpa's red brick, two-story building at the northeast end of the main street that housed Smith Implement Company has been raised. We always drive around town when we make our Memorial Day trek to Lamont. Most of the houses are still right where they were and quite recognizable to me. However, even though I reminisce as to who lived in each one, I know that none of those people are still there.

Sadly, the generations before us died off and my contemporaries and their kids and grandkids moved on. It's human nature to think we need to move up in size from our birth town. Kids my age took the big plunge to Waterloo and Cedar Rapids when we graduated from high school. My kids graduated high school in Cedar Rapids and couldn't bear the thought of remaining in that little town. I wonder where Olivia and Nolan will go from Kansas City and what bigger place than Milwaukee will attract Carter?

Over the years I've answered the question, "where are you from" a million times. For several years I proudly said Lamont. Year by year, the responses grew dimmer. So I began saying a small town in Northeast Iowa. If that interested people enough to inquire further, I would identify Lamont as between Dubuque and Waterloo or near Backbone State Park. The "I see" was really weak so eventually I found myself saying, I'm from Iowa. People can't seem to remember that and are compelled to ask if I came from Ohio or Idaho. So now, I'm from the Midwest.

Jokes abound about Iowa. I get pretty offended when people think we're still wearing bib overalls and carrying pitchforks. Others laugh at the size of Iowa—one third the population of New York City. Of course, "corn" is the center of most of the jokes. One slur particularly gets my goat. Food critics dub Iowa as the Jello capital of the world. So just for spite, I'm including a family-favorite jello salad recipe from Bertha Shephard, long time Iowa farm wife and excellent cook.

7-up Salad

2 pkgs lemon jello	1 1/2 cups small marshmallows
1 cup hot water	1 20 oz can crushed pineapple
1 cup cold water	3 bananas
2 cups 7-up pop	

In 9 x 13 dish dissolve jello in hot water. Mix in cold water and pop. Refrigerate until partially thickened. Fold in marshmallows and pineapple, drained well and reserved. Slice bananas to cover top. Cover dish with plastic wrap and refrigerate until set. Topping:

2 T butter	1 cup pineapple juice
2 T flour	1 beaten egg
1/2 cup sugar	1/2 cup whipped cream

Add water to reserved pineapple juice to make 1 cup. Cook above mixture over low heat stirring until thickened. Cool. Fold in whipped cream. Frost salad with topping and chill.

* * *

Iowa is a farm state supplying a major share of commodities to the world. While I was growing up, the countryside was filled with small farms averaging about 120 acres each. Farmers didn't make a lot of money but they were pretty self-sufficient. They grew corn, soybeans, oats and hay in their fields. The planting, cultivating, and harvesting kept them busy about eight months a year. The tractors were small having just replaced horses for power in the fields. I can remember

Grandpa Otterbeck walking in his cornfield behind a single-bladed plow pulled by two workhorses. Corn planters, plows, and corn pickers handled only two or four rows of corn at a time. Many of my classmates spent summers manning the equipment in the fields, if they were lucky. Otherwise, they had to walk beans, pick up rocks, or de-tassel corn. We all knew that corn had to be knee-high by the Fourth of July and picked by Thanksgiving. We watched for the rain in between and sweat through the hot days in August when you could hear the corn grow. When the harvested corn ran 100 bushels to the acre, everyone was happy. Big yields like that came about when manure was replaced by manufactured fertilizers.

Most farms had some milk cows to provide milk, cream, butter, and ice cream. They raised a few cattle and hogs to put beef and pork on the table. Many farmers butchered their own animals while others took the meat to a local locker to be processed. If they didn't have a freezer large enough to hold their meat, they would rent a locker in town to store it before taking it home in smaller quantities. Chickens were raised on every farm to provide eggs daily and, of course, the Sunday dinner. All we needed to do was catch a chicken, ring its neck, dip it in boiling water, pick off the feathers, and singe the pinfeathers before throwing it into the pot to cook. Sheep, goats, and horses rounded out the usual farmyard. Livestock not consumed by the farm family was sold to the stockyards, hopefully for a profit.

Every farm had a big garden so food could be canned or frozen for the winter months. The produce was stored in the cellar. Gardens were a source of pride as the long rows of sweet corn, tomatoes, green beans, peas, carrots, onions and potatoes lined up neatly with rich black weed-free soil between them. Grandma Otterbeck had a strawberry patch and most farms had berry bushes and fruit trees tucked away somewhere on their acreages. Raspberry jam, rhubarb crisp, and apple pie were but a few of the delicacies you could count on. Many farms had creeks and woods where mushrooms were hunted and fried for the special dinners in the springtime, and wood was chopped for the cooking and heating stoves.

Morning and evening every day of the year, cows had to be milked and animals had to be fed. Eggs had to be gathered and barns had to be cleaned. Many of the boys and some of the girls helped their Dads with chores before and after school. When I stayed overnight with Rita, she was relieved of chore duties by her sister Kay. Rita had to return the favor when Kay had a friend for a sleepover. Morning and evening chores were often completed in the dark; the snowstorms and minus-twenty-degrees weather didn't stop them either. In fact, it made it worse, because farmers had to keep water thawed so the animals could drink. The girls helped with the cooking, gardening, canning, laundry and house cleaning without the help of modern appliances. And some did it without running water, indoor plumbing and electricity.

I probably better clarify some things about the farming in my day. First, I wasn't one of those teens from the farm, and secondly, farming conditions improved following the war. The farms and the farm equipment were becoming larger and most farms had the modern conveniences thanks to the Rural Electric Cooperatives springing up in the forties. Fertilizers increased the crop yields and chemicals reduced the weeds. Feed additives hurried the weight gain on the livestock to get a quicker turnabout for market.

From age five to twelve, I lived in a new house in town with many of the modern conveniences that we take for granted today. The house had new furniture. The wood furniture was either bleached blonde or limed oak. The paint on the walls was colorful—dark teal and rose. Wallpaper adorned some of the walls. The kitchen table and chairs were chrome and padded plastic, just like the nostalgic pictures of the fifties depict.

The very, very best part of having a new house in town was the cement sidewalk running the width of the property in front of the house. Roller-skating on the sidewalks was a great pastime made even better by a sidewalk with no pits. Skates were of the metal variety that clipped onto shoes. The substantial brown high tops with the wide leather sole worked the best for holding the clamps of the skates. The shoes weren't too cool, but the shoestring hanging around the neck to secure the skate key to tighten the clamps was cool. The skates, the key, and I glided endlessly back and forth on the smooth sidewalk with nothing but dreams to interrupt young thoughts.

From town, we moved to a small acreage outside of Lamont where I lived for the rest of my days before marriage. Grandpa had horses and ponies, twenty or thirty at a time, but we didn't depend on the farm for our livelihood. I had my own pony but riding was of NO interest to me. We also had a peacock and a peahen. The peacock strutted around the yard spreading its wings many times daily, pretty as a picture. Farming was part of our lives through Grandpa's implement business and through the lives of most of my friends and classmates. If a family didn't farm directly, they still depended on farmers for their income because they hauled cattle to market like Skin Estling did, hauled milk to the creamery like Bob Adams, or had a business like Verbugt's grocery store where the farm families shopped and had their meat cut up and stored in the lockers.

Today the independent farms have been gobbled up; about one out of four—if that many—farmsteads remain. The big farms of 1000 acres and more are no longer diverse. Most either raise hundreds of acres of one crop per year or specialize in raising one kind of meat on the hoof in large herds. There are some dairy farms and some chicken farms all producing large quantities of food. Farming is a huge, complicated business and no longer only a means of self-sufficiency. Some smaller farmers and their wives have full time jobs off the farm. Many of the farms are corporations, some owned by foreign investors, without farm buildings or homes for families to occupy.

The red wooden barns, hog houses, chicken coops, machine sheds, and corn bins from my childhood are practically extinct. The farm where I lived as a little girl has been leveled, now serving only as a home for crops. If the buildings on farmland have been replaced, they are usually made of metal. The land has been cleared of all woods, tree groves, and rocks in an effort to make the land totally usable for crop production. It appears that each house is allotted two trees for shade. Fences are gone that once marked the small farms since there are no animals to keep in or out, as Frost eluded to in his poem, *Fences*.

Driving through Iowa, travelers see wide expanses of land with nothing to dot the landscape. A farmstead complete with a house and five or six out buildings used to lie every quarter mile or so along the old dirt roads.

I was a townie and I knew all the other townspeople. Today, it irritates me when I read or hear a name mentioned as a Lamont resident. If I don't know them, I always say they aren't really from Lamont. I dropped my subscription to *The Lamont Leader* since familiar names were no longer making the news. I could still name who used to live in every house and tell you a lot of stories about each family. Maybe half of it was gossip but probably most of it was founded in truth. Every house had its skeletons but none were buried deep enough to keep them hidden.

However, I came to know that every person has worth. Every person deserves a friendly smile, a heartfelt greeting, and some idle chitchat regarding a shared commonality, even if it's only the weather. That's the lesson I learned from all my hometown folks. Most all are dead now, but their friendliness and acceptance live forever through the lessons their lives taught me.

Steve Ivory always struck up "Mary, Mary, quite contrary, how does your garden grow" when I passed by the plumbing shop in the middle of main street. And lots of times I saw him running up the alley when the fire whistle blew to summon the volunteers. He and Lillian didn't have any children, but it didn't spare them from friendliness to everybody else's kids.

Dorothy McBride didn't have any children either and she was the nicest person a kid would ever want to meet. She always called me Deedle. To the rest of Lamont, I was Merry Dee. When she would see me coming down the street she would extend her hand as an invitation for me to walk along with her—just for a chat.

Dorothy and Lillian were both telephone operators. They let me watch them work in the telephone office connecting the locals who wanted to talk to each other. They answered "Operator" and pushed and pulled cords in the middle of our conversation without ever missing a word or a smile.

Fred was one of the town characters. Sometimes kids would make fun of him. There was nothing wrong with him. He was just too poor to buy food or keep clothes clean or new. He walked around town pulling a two-wheeled cart (Tevia style) to pick up food discarded behind the grocery stores. Sometimes he was behind the school rummaging through the hot lunch garbage. Since kids taunted him so often, he never looked up or spoke to them. But I copied Grandpa one day and said, "How ya doin', Fred." He flashed a toothless smile and said, "Purdy good."

I named one of my Christmas townspeople Frederick, after him. He has patched clothing and carries a goose in a basket. Fred probably never had a goose for Christmas, but I thought he should have. I named two of the other gift-carrying statues Francille and Lawrence after Doc and Fran. The fourth one is playing a musical instrument. I named him Archibald after the old man who came around a couple times a year to tune our piano.

Doc always called me Betty Grabel because he said I looked like her. I'm sure I didn't, but that didn't stop me from busting my buttons. Grandpa O called me Shaggy. I liked that, too. I guess that's why I have pet names for people. "Terms of Endearment", you might say, beginning way back in Lamont. I used to call Beth "Fuzzy Britches". We all called Eve "Beve", "Bease" and "Beaser" because Beth thought Eve's name should begin with the "B" sound like hers. I also called both girls Tallulah or Tilly Magoo or Missy. Beth didn't like being called Buelah, but that's who she was when her hair was a mess.

As long as I am digressing, I might as well talk about our cars' names. Cars need names. We have to call them something when we talk to them or even about them. We've had Soupy so named because he was the Super Sport model. Ralph was an Oldsmobile named after the salesman. Grace was another Oldsmobile, the female parked beside Ralph in the garage. Our first Honda had to be named Wanda for the rhyme. When we got her mate, we named him Irwin, to complete the couple that began with my friend Wanda from Lamont. When I got the Acura Legend, he was named Ichabod, referring to the *Legend of Sleepy Hollow*. The Honda Civic Hatchback had a big rear end so she became Bertha (Big Butt). Recently we got a new red car and Sid and I looked at each other and said simultaneously, let's call her Ruby. One note here: I'm not the only one who's a little dippy. Our friends and family called our cars by their given names also. And Olivia could recite our family history of cars when she was five—cars we had forty years before she was born.

Back to Lamont. I can cover one-half of the town by talking about the Wessels and Helms families who became connected through marriage. If I recall correctly, Ed Wessels married Lillian Helms and they had somewhere around ten kids. I used to be able to name them in order. It went something like Babe, Ladd, Butch, Deets, Larry, Dick, Carmen, Diane and Debbie. Lillian had two brothers—George and Bernie. They both reared their families in Lamont, also. I think George and Ila had about as many kids as the Wessels. They had Russell, Marilyn, Darwin, Georgia, Dawn, Beverly, Chip, and a couple more. Bernie had only about five children—four girls and a boy, I think. Anyway, these three families of first cousins were my contemporaries. They were all fun loving and mischievous characters that loved to dance and party. They made up about half of the basketball team, half of the town and half of the Catholic Church. For a lot of years, I thought, like the rest of the Methodists, that the party traits belonged to Catholics exclusively, particularly because they were the only church with a dance hall that sold beer. To this day, when I see someone having a good time, I am reminded of the Wessels and Helms families from Lamont.

Catholics in the forties and fifties weren't supposed to be practicing birth control; apparently the word reached Lamont. Doc and Fran were Catholics who produced an only child—Mary Beth. Doc often told the story of sitting in church and hearing the priest say, "If you have only one child, you might as well kill the one you have." Evidently the plot was to replace yourself and more.

Another large family was the Kremers who had six boys and six girls. Their first cousins were the Bergfelds who had six or more kids. A large part of the church was made up of Goedkens. I'll bet there were a hundred first and second cousins. And I can't forget the Kochs of which there were several large families, all related. Koch in Lamont was pronounced coke. Pepsi Koch was a girl in a class just a few years behind me. As my world broadened, I was surprised to discover that Koch rhymed with cook some places. Then Mayor Koch of New York thought his name was pronounced Kotch. I'm convinced one of his ancestors who couldn't spell must have lost the t just like Brett Favre's ancestors transposed the v and the r.

Two huge events occurred in Lamont while I lived there. One was the bank robbery. A gun-wielding robber herded Banker Emil Barz and several other locals into the bank vault one snowy winter afternoon. The robber escaped with about $4000 in cash and, to my knowledge, is still on the loose. That was fifty years ago so I guess he could be dead, and for sure, he's spent the money. Grandpa always claimed the robber escaped in a delivery truck that had left the shop. He thought two men were in the truck as it headed out of town, but only one had been seen in the truck before the robbery. That theory was never proven so the great Lamont bank heist remains an unsolved mystery.

The other big deal was the centennial. Lamont was founded in the 1850s; we had a great time celebrating her 100th birthday. The party lasted several days. We girls were all decked out in bonnets and bloomers. The ladies wore long dresses covering their petticoats and donned big old chapeaus. The men grew beards and most found a pair of suspenders to wear for at least one day of partying. The Bulldog marching band with Majorette Judy Wessels and the big bass drum advertising "Lamont" lead the noisy parade down the main street. Old Model "T" Fords, horses ridden by the Lamont Saddle Club, donkeys, goats, and screaming little kids filled the parade route. A carnival big enough to bring a Ferris Wheel to town was busy at one end of the street. Every church had a food stand with home baked pies and cakes served with ice cream from a hand-cranked freezer. Both big and little kids were kept busy with baseball games during the day. At night, a street dance revealed old folks with hands pumping up and down and young kids rockin' and rollin' right in the middle of the street. Plenty of other games like the Dunkin' Stand dropped Tracy Donaldson or other favorite citizens into the horse tank brimming with ice cold water. Those same tanks held orange pop for the women and kids and plenty of beer for the men and boys who could sneak off with a bottle of brew. Contests to judge the longest beards, the fanciest hats, and everything in between were held on the hour all afternoon. Some historians wrote and read the town's history that didn't interest me then, but it sure does now.

When I graduated from high school, it was time to leave Lamont. I thought I was all grown up, but I know now that the seeds had only been sown. I've also figured out that I'll probably never really grow up. There's something about being a kid …

GO YE BULLDOGS

I graduated from Lamont High School. We were the Bulldogs clad in orange and black singing "Go Ye Bulldogs, Go Ye Bulldogs, fight and win this game" to the tune of *On Wisconsin*. A couple of years later, Lamont merged with Strawberry Point and Arlington to become Starmont High School. And the Bulldogs became Stars. Grandpa Smith was against the merger saying that it would be the demise of Lamont. He was right, in that it was the beginning of change from the Lamont I had known.

    The big German Catholic farm families are no longer. However, they make up a large part of my memory since many were classmates from first through twelfth grade. I started first grade and finished twelfth grade with Georgia Helms, Ray Helms, Lawrence Gruman, Donnie Ovel, Dick Estling, David Berns, Larry Steffen, Linda Bergfeld, Laura Ann Kremer and Patty Slater. Jon Downer, Larry Streicher, Willis Brewer, Janet Stewart, Wanda Hotchkiss, Keith McCallum, Dianne

Colton, John Parmely, Ronnie Ives, and Mae Sheldon were the other half on the protestant side. We all started and ended our schooling together.

Several other classmates were with us for a long time. We had two Sandy's—Sandy King and Sandy Scheiss. They had short statures in common as well. Linda Ehlers upped the ante of Linda's to two. At graduation, we had four guys named Larry—Steffen, Streicher, Gaffney and Reiling. Only two of them started off with us in first grade and only two of them were ever my boyfriends.

Dennis Dake, Bobby Walsh, Sharon Beaman, Karen Pospisil, Rita Carpenter, Judy Anderson, Jerry Heyer, and Darwin Helms were around for so much of our schooling that they seem like lifetime classmates as well. How could I forget Darwin who pulled my chair back just as I was about to sit down for our reading group in the little closet just off Miss Hole's 3rd grade classroom? Kerplunk.

Jerry Recker, Walter Koch, and Kenneth Linderwell were farm kids from Lamont who were part of my grade school classes. Other grade school kids who moved on were Roger Nelson, whose father was a Methodist minister, and Steve Elliot who stayed around Lamont and was my date for prom our senior year. I was dating Danny at the time, but he wasn't the prom type. To complicate things regarding men and my senior prom, Sid and I danced together for the first time at that prom. Records provided the music—no DJ or band expected.

The official name was the Junior-Senior Banquet and Prom. The festivities began with a full meal cooked by mothers and served by freshmen and sophomores in the school cafeteria. The dance was in the gym that was unrecognizable because the walls and ceiling were covered with strips of twisted crepe paper. Even the paint stripes marking the basketball court were covered up. Fake green grass from the local mortuary did that trick. The whole affair was a project of the junior class, which meant we attended as juniors and were the special guests as seniors.

At first we didn't have any Diana's in our class and then we had two. Diana Tegler joined us in high school since her country grade school ended with eighth grade. Joe Goedken came with her. Diana was a huge boost to the music department. I was lucky enough to be paired with her as the alto in a quartet completed with Alan Becker and Marvin Cumberland. I give Diana the credit for getting us to All State Chorus. She was definitely All State material and I wasn't, but I enjoyed the trip to Des Moines. Diana Nelson was a big asset to our basketball team after the neighboring town of Aurora no longer had a high school. I think that school closing is how we got Linda Werner, too. I'm not sure how we ended up with Bill Whitman in our class, but we did, and that was a good thing.

Most of the boys in my class were my boyfriend at sometime or other. Donnie Ovel gave me a pencil box for Christmas one year. I still have the paper, bow, and tag in a scrapbook. Lawrence Gruman was my cousin's boyfriend and we formed a foursome with his older brother John as my boyfriend. Our relationship lasted three years until we moved to the farm. When we were no longer neighbors, it wasn't a convenience to be hooked up with the Gruman boys. I liked Jon Downer several different times throughout grade school. That doesn't mean, though, that he liked me. Janet's boyfriends were my boyfriends, too, so I put Bobby Walsh and Ray and Darwin Helms on my boyfriend list.

David Berns was extra kind to everyone. He was shy and bashful—something of which I was never accused. Dickie Estling swallowed a marble in fourth grade; either Miss Edna or Miss Erma picked him up and held him upside down by the heels until he spit it out. Another time Miss Erma made me stay in from recess because I hadn't completed my math assignment. I told her that I had finished it and put it on her desk but someone must have stolen it. I implicated Ronnie Ives. I'm sure Miss Erma and Ronnie both knew I was telling a fib, but I don't recall being chastised by either one.

All the girls in my class were at one time or other my best friends. Kids are awfully fickle when it comes to "best friends". I remember overnights with Patty, Rita, and Wanda. Wanda was full of musical talent and Rita epitomized the work ethic on the family farm. Patty and

I often ended up next to each other in classes since our last names were linked alphabetically. May Sheldon was in my 4-H group so I used to see her on Saturdays, also.

One of my best girl friends, Marlene Glass, moved away from Lamont when we were in sixth grade. I visited her in Wisconsin the summer after she left. The trip was memorable on its own accord, but more so because I collected my first recipe from my godmother on a side trip to her Wisconsin home. She served Sloppy Joes that I thought were delicious. I asked her for the recipe that I still have in my youthful handwriting. I've passed it on more than any other in my files, but then, I've had it more than fifty years. Some people call them Maidrites or Loose Meat but our family calls them *Taverns*, a colloquialism we picked up in Western Iowa.

Taverns

2 T butter	1/2 cup water
2 T vinegar	1 cup catsup
2 T brown sugar	1 chopped onion
3 T Worchestershire	salt
1 tsp mustard	pepper

Mix the above ingredients and let simmer 30 minutes. Meanwhile, simmer 2 pounds of hamburger in small amount of water with seasoning. Drain when browned. Add sauce to hamburger and simmer 15 minutes. Fills 12 hamburger buns.

*   *   *

Janet was my very best friend all the way through school. We did everything together, except cry over homework. She shed real tears when she couldn't solve her algebra problems. That always amazed me; I would never waste my tears on algebra. I was the leader in that twosome. I had already learned to boss people around by the time we became friends.

On my sixth birthday in first grade, I convinced Janet during afternoon recess that it was time to go home. I was pretty sure that my present was a new bicycle and I couldn't wait to see it. We walked to my house and sure enough, there it sat all shiny and blue, just waiting for me in the garage. Janet's Dad almost beat us home after receiving the phone call that we were missing from school. We never skipped out again.

I didn't know how to ride a bike so I waited until Terry got home from school. He took the first ride and headed straight into a tree on the Cowles property next door. The collision smashed the light on the front fender so I really never had the perfect new bike I dreamed about. The light was never replaced and eventually the bottom shell of the light rusted out from water sitting in it. I rode that bike to its demise that occurred about the same time I started driving Grandpa's green Oldsmobile.

"Going Steady" was a common occurrence among teen-agers. That meant you had exchanged class rings and weren't dating anyone else at the time—unless you thought you could get by with it. The coolest thing was wrapping angora string around the boy's ring to make it fit the girl's finger. Actually, you could go steady before you had a class ring, as long as the guy had access to a car. And going steady didn't always have a lot of longevity with it. I can't remember everyone I went steady with, and for fear I would embarrass them, I won't name names. It is here in some situations that people would say, "You know who you are." But some of them might not due to short memories, denial, or whatever. Beth Ford always said that she picked up with my old boyfriends when I had finished with them. What a hoot.

Each night after school we hung out at Hayford's Drug Store. Janet, Ray Helms and I often joined friends from other classes. I always had a five-cent fountain coke and a Walnut Crush Candy Bar. Sometimes I splurged on a Dusty Road Sunday which was vanilla ice cream topped with chocolate sauce and malt powder. Like the rest of the Midwest, we drank pop, not soda, and we carried it out of the store in a sack, not a bag.

After the drug store, my next stop was the shop. Grandpa's implement business was my part time job from the time I was twelve years old. I sorted through the sales receipts for the day to remove the sold parts from inventory. During Christmas vacation, I helped count the entire inventory. Bins of nuts, bolts, burrs, washers and corn picker chain links still stick in my mind and the grease stuck on my fingers for longer than I wished. Grandpa was the Allis Chalmers, New Idea, and Massy Harris dealer. I learned quite a bit about farm implements during that time. I knew the difference between WC and WD tractors and that corn planters had shoes—but no feet. Incidentally, there is no connection to plantars warts or the corns that pester feet.

Especially during the wintertime, farmers hung around the shop for hours. I picked up on how men talk and think and haggle as they leaned first on one foot and then the other. I didn't realize at the time that I was gleaning negotiating skills that helped me cross the gender barrier throughout my career.

Teens were not faced with the tough temptations like kids since the fifties have experienced. We were spared partly because of the small town we lived in but mostly because of the era. We didn't have gangs or drugs as a threat. Most of us didn't smoke or drink beer in high school. Racing around in cars—and what you did in the back seat—was about the extent of our mischievous behavior. Cars meant drag races, doing donuts at the end of the main street, and occasional parking on dark lonely roads after a movie or a school event. Lamont had no stoplights and I'm pretty sure it never will. A rolling stop was all it took at the first stop signs installed shortly before I got my driver's license.

Drive-ins were the rage. Weekends we trekked off to a drive-in movie, sometimes several carloads together. No one watched the movie. We ate, gossiped, scanned the rows for acquaintances, checked out the cool cars, and watched windows steam up. More often, the drive-in was a restaurant. All the bigger towns (population one or two thousand) offered at least one drive-in where we hung to check out cars, couples, and anything in between. Breaded pork tenderloins, as big as a dinner plate, bulged out of oversized buns. A and W Root Beer or a malted milk usually washed down the snack. In the winter when the drive-ins weren't open, we often went to Maryville for a hamburger before taking the long road home through Backbone and scooping the main street in Lamont for any action.

Being a teenager in the famous fifties decade is one of my greatest claims to fame. Rock and Roll and Elvis were my era. I watched Elvis Presley on his first television appearance on the *Ed Sullivan Show*. Lots of kids were forbidden to watch because of his gyrating hips. I swooned throughout *Love Me Tender,* his first major movie, when it opened in Des Moines. We watched Dick Clark's *American Bandstand* and followed the lives of the dancers. Sandy was my favorite.

We wore poodle skirts, saddle shoes, hoop underskirts, see-through nylon blouses, cardigans, fake angora collars, and pearls. We starched our petticoats so they could stand up by themselves. The coolest guys had button-down shirts and Ivy League buckles on the back of their trousers.

The boys sported ducktails and combed their hair up on the sides to form a curl in the center of their foreheads. The girls set their hair on rollers, not the bobby-pin sets like our mothers. We held our "do" with a dishtowel wrapped around our head while waiting for the locks to dry. Then we backcombed our hair to stand up and circle our heads like a steel helmet. I went to the beauty shop once a week to get my hair done. I never combed through it all week until the next appointment. Weekly baths were often coordinated with the weekly shampoos. Just about the only place showers could be found was in the school locker rooms. A few houses had showers in the basement.

School events kept us out of trouble. Events included girls' and boys' basketball games, school plays, FHA, FFA and FBLA meetings, school newspaper and annual work nights, band and chorus concerts, and most anything else to get us out of the house. We had slumber parties on the weekends and sleepovers during the week.

Our dates took us to a movie or the roller rink on weekends. The luckiest kids owned their roller skates toted in a brightly colored suitcase with metal corners. Huge yarn pompons to match our outfits were attached to the bottom laces of the skates. I rented my skates, but to satisfy my vanity, I attached the pompons that I brought from home.

Janet would sometimes drive her Mom's Volkswagen Beetle, a new import on the car scene during our teen years. One time we parked it near the white bridge in Lamont only to find it moved crosswise of the ditch when we returned. Jon Downer and friends finally quit laughing and came out from under the bridge to lift it back to the side of the road.

Looking back from the other side of the desk, I understand the role that my small town played in my education. The "pick of the crop" teachers did not come to rural towns like Lamont if circumstances would allow them to go elsewhere—particularly to a bigger town. Most of the good ones that we had were there because they were born there, lived near there, or married someone who lived there. The curriculum was limited. There were only four science courses, and until we were freshmen, students couldn't take algebra if enrolled in band because of the schedule conflict. Art classes weren't taught by certified art teachers at any level in our school and the only language taught was first-year German. Instructional techniques were limited to assignments page by page out of the textbook. As far as I can remember, we were all Caucasian, Christian, and American. Other cultures were something belonging to someone else, somewhere else.

We have the distinction of being the last class to graduate from Lamont without having kindergarten. Lamont started kindergarten in 1948 when my class entered school. Using age and readiness testing for criteria, half of us went into first grade and half went to kindergarten. Therefore, I always thought we had smart kids in our class. Probably the truth is, most of us went to first grade because we were too old for kindergarten.

Rita and I hooked up for education again after high school. I rushed to get my Bachelor degree in three years. Rita wasn't much later receiving her teaching degree from UIU. Janet attended Iowa State and finished her Medical Technology preparations at Baylor University. Dennis Dake succeeded as head of the Art Department at Iowa State. He was in the military after high school before getting his degree in art. I asked him how he could excel in art with no formal art education in high school at Lamont. He gave Willis Brewer the credit for his inspiration.

After twelve years of school together, the bonds were pretty strong. The down side of being with the same thirty kids for all the growin' up years is that they know EVERYTHING. I confessed to some things in this book that I otherwise wouldn't have, but I knew that Jon and Larry, among others, would give me a lot of grief for not fessing up. I hope my memory is mostly correct and that I didn't omit or wrongfully categorize anyone. We'll soon be getting together for our fifty-year class reunion to rekindle friendships and share versions of Bulldog recollections. My memory will probably be in for a challenge.

MARRIAGE MADE IN HAVOC

Marriage accounts for two-thirds of my life so far. Ye Gads, that's a long time. No wonder the initial spark flickers now and then. Some wise sage (I think it was Uncle Bill) once pointed out that no species except the human race tries to co-inhabit with the same person for decades. Certainly, most others, lions come to mind, go with a one-night-stand. So far we've had roughly 15,000 one-nighters and have lived to tell about it.

We met my senior year of high school. I was a student and Sid was the new band director just out of college. He tried early in the year to bolster the band numbers (sixteen when he arrived) and asked me to rejoin the band. I had quit my sophomore year because my boyfriend Larry was in study hall during the band period which was much more enticing than the clarinet. I didn't take the new band director up on his offer.

I was, however, active in vocal groups and chorus my senior year so that took me to the gym/stage area that served as the room for vocal music. Instrumental music used the stage, also, as well as the one-room schoolhouse that was just out the stage door. So our paths often crossed. Sid made the mistake of telling a student and friend, Maury Dake, that he was going to take me out after I graduated. That piqued my interest, even though I was "going steady" during my senior year.

We had our first date one week after high school graduation. Sid fixed up a double date with my friend, Janet, and his friend, Lee. We went to a dance at the Coliseum Ballroom in Oelwein. Janet and I were both seventeen and our dates were twenty-two. Not a problem except, the guys were used to drinking and we weren't. This was before liquor-by-the-drink in Iowa. So the guys ordered setups and supplied the bourbon from a flask. We tried to act like we knew what we were doing; somehow we kept our wits about us, never thinking about under-age drinking.

We went our separate ways for the summer. Before I left for college in the fall, we had our first solo date, again to a dance. In October, Sid invited me to go to the homecoming dance at Upper Iowa. That Friday night when I arrived home for the weekend my relationship ended with the current boyfriend as he and his friends came in one driveway and Sid came in the other. Frost's "The Road Not Taken" comes to mind.

The romance went on with visits back and forth between Des Moines and Lamont until I transferred to Upper Iowa in January. Sid was still teaching in Lamont and I was living on campus. Every weekend we went to a dance or to a nightclub for dinner and dancing to live bands. That was our entertainment—eating, drinking, dancing. Not much has changed in forty-five years.

The fling probably would have ended if not for Fran Ford. One October afternoon while sitting on her sofa, she suggested Sid and I should look at the cute little house for rent that was visible from her window. It was a story-and-a-half house painted beige—or pink, according to some people. The kitchen was knotty pine and a bonus feature was a detached single-stall garage.

We had never had a discussion about getting married, but we went to look at the house anyway. We liked the house and told the owners we would take it. The owner asked if we were married; we said no. We should have added that we weren't engaged, either, and further, we hadn't even thought about it.

I don't remember the conversation the rest of that evening but the next day after the football game at Upper Iowa, we went to Oelwein to select my engagement ring. Grandpa and Grandma attended the game with us to watch the Lamont band march at half time of the game. Beth Ford was the majorette for the band that had grown to about thirty players. We managed to get back to the house for dinner that evening to announce our engagement. It had been a busy day.

The next morning (Sunday) the jeweler at Kappmeyer's opened his store so we could pick up the rings. With the diamond still in the box, we decided to stop at Sid's Grandma Gray's house while in Oelwein to tell her of our upcoming marriage. We pulled into the ally and parked in the garage since she was away at church. At that point, the question was asked and before I answered, I heard, "Of course you will." I never have answered that question.

The next item on the agenda was a wedding. I thought a Christmas wedding would be wonderful. Sid, however, refused, because he had plunked down $50 for a month's rent for the house and he was going to live in it. No amount of haggling would change his mind. So we got married on Thanksgiving weekend with superb help and organization from Aunt Maybelle. I dropped Merry Dee, the name she had given me, and became Merry C.

In the middle of planning the wedding, we had to furnish our house. That went pretty smoothly except for buying the appliances. We chose the refrigerator and gas range that we needed to "set up housekeeping". On the side, I told the salesman to deliver the portable dishwasher that Sid had ignored during the shopping spree.

As luck would have it, I wasn't at the house when the appliances were delivered. Sid told the deliverymen they had made a mistake; the dishwasher needed to go back. When I showed up at the house, I was dismayed to find that I didn't have a dishwasher. After a brief discussion, I said that I didn't intend to begin doing dishes just because

I was getting married. Sid said he would do them rather than buy the dishwasher. I responded, "It's a deal." Three years and dozens of broken dishes later, he finally relented.

A Kirby vacuum cleaner was one of the other initial purchases that we made when we got married. Forty-five years later we still have the same Kirby that has logged thousands of hours and been reconditioned only once. After Beth and Eve had their own homes, they each requested a Kirby for Christmas. We got them each a second-hand vacuum cleaner as new ones by this time were pretty pricey. Theirs will probably last a lifetime, also.

Our one-night honeymoon was at the Town House Hotel in Cedar Rapids followed by shopping at Armstrong's the next day. Upon returning to Lamont it was obvious that our house had been ransacked. A picnic table was turned on end to block the front door.

My first task when entering the house was to go to the bathroom. I had waited all day to peel the knee-length girdle off under the tight sheath dress. That accomplished, I noticed no sound and soon discovered that my clothes around my ankles were getting wet. Saran Wrap had been put over the toilet stool. As I attempted to wash my hands, there was no water; the soap was covered with clear fingernail polish. Meanwhile, Sid was discovering other Tom Foolery. That evening the Ford Family showed up with clanking pans for a serenade and our reaction to their stunts. Fran complained the rest of her life that her pans were damaged during those escapades.

Uncle Bill had informed us in the afternoon that the teachers were coming to shivaree us that evening. We would need beer. Since Sid was a teacher in Lamont, he could not go into the tavern to buy beer. Bill offered to make the purchase. Of course, it was Uncle Bill and the rest of my family and the Fords who showed up that night to drink the beer.

The next morning, I was determined to get off on the right foot by cooking breakfast for my new husband. We sat down to our first meal in our new home and Sid's first response was, "Well, you can forget this." Apparently the bacon and eggs were overcooked a little. So I took him at his word, and have never (i.e. never, ever) cooked breakfast for him since.

A few nights later we were shivareed by the teachers. I was attending night class and Sid was in bed naked and asleep when two women pulled him out of bed. When I arrived home, we fed the guests the layer of wedding cake that had been saved in the freezer for that very purpose. This group, also, had fun with the house. Labels were taken off cans, salt was sprinkled in bedroom drawers, and the bed was short-sheeted.

We did our share of shivareeing other newly weds. I remember when a bunch of us—mostly classmates—invaded Rita and LaVerne's apartment. Prankster Darwin put salt in the sugar canister. I often wondered what Grandma Stoeckel, my former baby sitter, must have thought when we arrived at her upstairs apartment to shivaree fellow teacher Fred Clark and his new wife.

The first year and a half of our marriage was consumed with finishing college. I earned a Bachelor of Science degree with my first major in Business Education. My second major was English with a minor in Speech. I attended classes all year round to graduate in three years. I was twenty in August of 1963 when I walked across the stage to get my diploma.

A week later we moved to Lake Mills where Sid was the band director and I began my teaching career in high school English. Some students were eighteen years old, just two years younger than I. Emmitt Brower was the high school principal. He told me before that first day of school that I had better be tough and set some strict guidelines. Reports were immediate that I got my point across. Thanks to Mr. Brower, I wasn't plagued with discipline problems during my career.

When I became pregnant with Beth near the end of my first year of teaching, I went to Superintendent Mitchell to resign. The time had come for me to stay home and raise kids. The Superintendent, however, said he preferred that I take a semester leave of absence and continue teaching. He needed me to teach composition, something that was not prevalent with other teachers at the time. At that pivotal point three years after our wedding, I was off and running with a family and a career, the stuff of later chapters.

I've put a bunch of work over the years in trying to perfect my first husband even though I've read many times that changing a man's habits can't be easily accomplished. I think I have him trained pretty well for his next wife. But I will tell you, he still has some short comings: he doesn't dust the top of the refrigerator, he sorts laundry by type rather than color, he won't use Pledge, he vacuums everything dead or alive, he falls asleep watching television, he snorts when he blows his nose, and he bumps his head creating a new scar at least once a month.

We had a zillion happy experiences shared with wonderful friends and family. We went through all the trials and tribulations that jobs, kids, and married life threw our way. We learned new habits and tried to unlearn old ones. We grew together and we grew a part. We remembered much and forgot more. We rejoiced over the good and regretted the bad. We mended broken hearts, and we survived.

THE BEGETING OF KIDS

Long before I was married and dreaming about adulthood as all teenage girls do, I knew what constituted a perfect family—two daughters was the answer. Some of the families I admired most consisted of two girls. My godmother and mother's close friend Evelyn had Charlotte and Barbara. Doc and Gaby's children were Janet and Nancy. Aunt Maybelle's two daughters were my cousins, Marilyn and Jacquie.

So when we were expecting, our first baby would be a girl. I never thought anything else. Sid was fine with having a daughter, if he had to have children at all. He would have preferred neither a boy nor a girl. Someone once asked me what if the baby turned out to be a boy. I said I would send it back. Fortunately, I didn't have to. Beth was what I wanted. Her name, Beth Janann, came from three friends. Mary Beth and Janet were childhood friends and Ann was a college friend.

When it was time for a second child to enter the scene, I again knew the baby needed to be a girl. However, Sid wanted a boy this time. I won the argument and delivered Eve. Sid was unhappy for a few hours but soon got over it. Her name was chosen from a list of credits on a TV soap opera. I had three miscarriages along the way. They must have been the boys. Someone was granting my wish for two girls.

Today, couples talk about being pregnant. Sid was not pregnant—I was. It didn't hinder smoking or drinking. I had no ultra sound to determine the baby's wellness, to say nothing of gender. I didn't take any nutrients or eat any special diet. I had my teeth x-rayed. The girls were healthy and remained healthy even though they didn't have car seats, let alone cars with seat belts or air bags. They rode their bikes and skateboards without helmets. Our houses didn't have furniture bolted to the walls, drawers kid proofed, or smoke detectors. We didn't put the medicine out of reach or use childproof caps. Water was safe to drink and not even a wacko would pay for water in a bottle. Packaging didn't deter kids from opening them, and warning labels, if printed at all, didn't take all the fun out of eating the product. Sunglasses and sunscreen never interfered with a day in the sun. Today, I would probably be arrested for child endangerment.

Delivering babies was an easy thing for me. I evidently inherited that gene from my mother. Doc Ford told me Mom planned to have a dozen kids. Eve had simple deliveries, also, so between the two of us, we assured Beth that delivering Carter would be a breeze. Maybe that wasn't the case.

The girls and their toddler years were the favorite part of my life. They were precious little blondes who were really good kids, once Eve stopped crying when she neared two years old. We never knew why she was unhappy, but thankfully it ended. Being teachers, we had three months to spend with the kids each summer. Looking back, that was a real blessing. We sacrificed a free trip to Europe chaperoning the band because it would have taken three weeks out of our summer with the girls. Most of all, we wouldn't have been home to celebrate Eve's birthday.

We all went to school for a few years until Sid chose a different career path. Beth and Eve were good students. School was a snap for Eve and good behavior was always reported. Beth had to work a bit harder, and when she did, she was successful. She also spent a lot more time getting in and out of trouble.

Their middle and high school teen years were sunny years from my standpoint. I taught kids this age, so I had an inkling of what to expect. They had good grades and good times and good friends. Neither was without a few incidents that they would not want me to recall.

Both girls inherited their Dad's musical talent, but neither chose to study music beyond high school. Beth sat first chair while playing French horn all through high school and Eve was in the First Flute section. I spent many nights sitting in the car reading *The Cedar Rapids Gazette* by the dim light of the sun visor while they attended their private lessons. Both girls also took piano lessons. Beth's early teacher said she had unbelievable natural talent. Eve could transpose rather sophisticated music at the keyboard when she was in second grade. Eve continued taking lessons as a teen and therefore was awarded our piano when she moved to her first apartment. Neither Sid nor I played the piano much as we became busy with the girl's lives.

We snow skied together in Colorado every winter and boated and water-skied on the Mississippi River during the hot, muggy summers. We always had dinner together every evening with a table properly set, no radio or television blaring and no hats allowed. Perhaps keeping the family closeness is why we see the girls and their families several times a year even though Texas is hundreds of miles from either one of them.

Grandma Smith's Meatballs were routine on our menu; the tradition continues to be savored by her great, great grandchildren, especially Carter. He never knew Grandma, but he loves her meatballs.

Grandma Smith Meatballs

1 pound hamburger	2 T minced onion
1 can mushroom soup	1 egg
1/2 cup water	1/4 tsp salt
3/4 cup minute rice	dash of pepper

Mix soup and water. Set aside 3/4 of the mixture. Add the rest of the ingredients to the remaining 1/4 of soup mixture. Shape into 12 balls and brown in 1 T of shortening in a skillet. Drain off fat. Add soup mixture that was set aside. Cover skillet and cook slowly 15 minutes.

*   *   *

"Would you make potato salad" is the most common food request within our family. I never minded that, but I was challenged to write down the recipe when Beth and Eve started cooking. They enjoy making it for their families and friends now also. The ingredients are ordinary; the technique requiring hot potatoes is the difference. The pickle relish needs to be the homemade variety like I get from Bea's in Door County.

Potato Salad

7 eggs	1 T sugar
7 medium red potatoes, unpeeled	2 T milk
1 tsp salt	3 T sweet pickle relish
1/2 onion, chopped	1 tsp Accent
1 1/2 cups Hellman's mayonnaise	1 tsp Lowry's seasoning salt

Hard boil the eggs. Boil potatoes with skins in salted water. Meanwhile in a small mixing bowl, mix mayo, sugar, milk and pickle relish. Peel and chop eggs and place in a large mixing bowl. Add salt and onion. Drain potatoes when cooked and immediately (using hot pads) skin and chop the potatoes. Add to eggs and onion. Pour mayo mixture over top and stir while potatoes are still hot. Allow potatoes a couple minutes to absorb the mayo. Mix in Accent and Lowry's. Store covered in the refrigerator at least 3 hours before serving.

*   *   *

The girls' college years were a wonderful time for us. We were grateful to have both of them at the University because it was so close to Cedar Rapids. Seems like one or the other was coming or going most of the time to add a little variety to life's routine. We especially enjoyed tailgating with them and their friends during football season and attending the many parent events at their sorority house.

Both girls were given the same opportunity. They could go to the college of their choice—as long as it was a state university. One of OUR biggest accomplishments was THEIR completion of a Bachelors Degree in four years. Eve graduated with honors in the School of Education and Beth was chosen to represent the University at a Big Ten conclave of accounting graduates. Soon after, Beth obtained her CPA and Eve her Masters Degree.

We were also thankful that they both had secured their first jobs before graduation from Iowa. They mirrored each other by remaining to this day in the same cities where they chose to begin their careers twenty years ago. Beth headed off to Milwaukee where her career began in public accounting and continues with a banking corporation. Eve is still teaching in the public school district in the Kansas City suburb where she began her career. She has changed primary grade levels a few times as she juggled her career with having my grandchildren.

As the girls moved to their own places, I became an apartment and home decorator. They moved from apartment to apartment and then house to house and one, if not both of us, were there. We cleaned and scrubbed somebody else's dirt, cleaned up contractor's debris, painted walls and ceilings, wall papered, ripped off wallpaper, landscaped, shopped, shopped some more, returned what didn't suit, and literally delivered several rented U Hauls loaded with new furniture to Kansas City and Milwaukee. Without exaggerating, we have easily spent a whole year—a day and a week at a time—attending to their homes. Sid announced recently that he has put down the paintbrush for the final time. Beth has reached the age that I was when I started "doing" their apartments, so I think it is time to relinquish my role.

When weddings came along, I donned my wedding planner hat. Eve was first and complicated things by announcing her engagement in May and requesting an August wedding with the reception in our back yard. That wouldn't have been so bad except we had just moved into our new home in DeWitt and the yard wasn't landscaped yet. The backyard didn't even have grass. Sid took over the yard and it was beautiful by the wedding day. If this were his story, he would elicit all the problems he faced, but it isn't. Three weeks after the engagement announcement and with a wedding dress purchased, Eve left for Mississippi for her last summer of graduate school. She got back a week before her wedding. That left me with planning the affair; she did, however, make it easy by agreeing up front to the choices I would have to make in her absence.

We had given up on a wedding for Beth thinking that she had chosen her career over marriage. However, at thirty-five, she decided that the time had come. Her wedding was near Milwaukee so the major complication was the distance from Indianola. I vividly remember driving home alone in a blinding snowstorm after a day of wedding preparations. About two o'clock in the morning I finally gave up and checked into a motel in Iowa City. We enjoyed both girls' weddings and were happy we could host them.

So now I have two sons-in-law. That's a good thing. I didn't particularly think either one was what I had in mind for our girls, but they have proven me wrong. Grandma Smith didn't think Sid measured up to her expectations either. I recall her saying I should marry a king. I never asked her to defend her statement. Dave and Jon are great husbands and fathers, and like Sid, do their fair share of household chores and more. Both are appreciative of our family and don't make too many wise cracks about their mother-in-law.

The very best thing about having kids and weddings is that GRANDchildren usually follow.

Nolan came first. Again, I wanted a girl. But the day Nolan showed up, I went shopping and discovered that I could buy really cute clothes for boys. So I delivered a shopping bag full to the hospital. He must have liked his new clothes because we bonded that day and have been best buddies ever since.

My favorite picture of him is scooting across the floor to me before he could crawl. A great big grin is spread across his little face. You can't see me in the picture, but I know I am at the other end of his reach. I MIGHT be partial, but I don't think there is anyone but Nolan who says "Grandma" with such compassion in his voice. I've always thought Grandma's fell out of favor when little boys grew older, but he's ten now and my favorite big boy still calls me to chat and sends his hugs and kisses.

His external trademarks are his blond curls and his mismatched eyes—one blue and one gray/green. And I expect he will always be skinny. At this point he is a vegetarian. However, he has never eaten a vegetable unless ketchup and French fries qualify. He is bright and creative and has a sharp wit delivered by verbal skills that were obvious very early on. I have a basket full of his art and accompanying stories that he has designed since preschool. I suspect he will do well in life as he certainly has learned the art of manipulation from extended practice on his Grandma. I reward him for each A he gets on his report card. Every fall he calls to let me know the price per A has gone up.

We visited Nolan's preschool on grandparents' day when he was two. We drove to Kansas City that morning and went directly to his classroom. There were about a dozen kids standing in a row at the front. We took our seats and began searching for him, to no avail. As I surveyed the group, I asked Sid out of the side of my mouth if he saw him, and he said no. About that time I saw a kid in a designer sweatshirt. I figured that had to be my GRANDchild, and sure enough, a little hand went up to wave as that familiar smile crossed his face. We were relieved. On reflection, I guess I was expecting my GRANDchild to have a crown on his head to set him apart from the rest.

Olivia came second and so I finally got my girl. I had suggested the name three years earlier when I thought Nolan was supposed to be a girl. This time, Dave said if I would quit talking about it, he thought Eve might go for the name. So I did, and she did. She added her own middle name, Meree, pronounced Marie from a combination of Merry and Dee. That scored a lot of points.

Olivia was born in 2000 and her initials are OO so we have OO from '00. This year is a VERY special birthday for her. On 07/07/07 she will be 7 years old. That's enough to claim 7 as my lucky number. This will be her golden of golden birthdays. The odds of this occurrence are pretty rare. One would have to be born in the first twelve years of a century and in the first twelve days of a month to hit these unusual digits before becoming thirteen years old.

Livvy, like her Mother, was a fussy baby. She would always cuddle with me watching my lips as I sang, "You are my Sunshine." It's the kind of thing you wish you had a penny for every time you sang it. As she got a bit older, she loved to have me paint her finger and toe nails and she especially liked high heeled shoes. She would listen to story after story about her mom when she was a little girl. She liked me to put her hair in Buffy tails just like I used to do with her Mom's hair.

My favorite little girl Olivia loves pink but always says purple is her favorite color—the same as her Grandma and Mom. She is tall and lithe and wears clothes really well. She moves beautifully and is a natural dancer—inherited, no doubt—from Papa Sid.

I'm not sure what Olivia inherited from me, but I've often recited the nursery rhyme to her that I heard lots of times in my childhood. (Oh oh, OO.)

> *There was a little girl who had a little curl*
> *Right in the middle of her forehead,*
> *When she was good she was very very good*
> *But when she was bad she was horrid.*

Livvy always loved looking at books and listening to anyone who would read to her. Junie B. Jones books were her favorite when she began to read in kindergarten. I gave her most of them to complete her collection plus a journal just like the one Junie B kept. Livvy enjoys writing; maybe the journal will continue to encourage her to record her thoughts.

My last GRANDchild born was Carter, my favorite little boy. It doesn't look like Carter will have brothers and sisters, but that's all right because Beth and Jon got it right the first time. In fact, he couldn't be more perfect. He's four now and the cutest little stinker that ever came along. He has pure white hair like his Mom had and has the shortest little legs possible.

But those legs really keep him on the move. Any kind of ball will do—soccer, football, baseball, or basketball. He has the uniforms and equipment for the sports and has already attended high school, college and pro games. He began swimming and ice-skating lessons when he was two. And he was already riding the waves on an inter-tube behind the boat when he was three. He claims golf is his very favorite thing to do. When he got miffed at me, he told me he wouldn't play golf with me anymore. That was a big punishment for him to dish out.

We attended Grandparents Day at his preschool when he was two. It was there we learned that he had already been introduced to popcorn so we could go to movies and enjoy the treat even though we were told that was a no-no. We had fun breaking the rules his mom had laid down for him. She even told him McDonalds was closed every time he wanted to go there, but it's never closed when Grandma is around. His mom isn't going to be able to pull the wool over his eyes much longer—another bright GRANDchild.

Carter doesn't like to talk on the phone—not even to his Grandma. So I send him e-mails. Recently his Dad was at the computer and told him that he had an e-mail from Grandma Merry. He said," Well, it better be good." He's a big tease. I asked him to save me the purple jelly beans from his Easter basket. He sent me a picture with his grin from ear to ear, his mouth dripping purple, and a plate filled with every color of jelly bean, except purple.

We were called to duty to baby-sit all of the GRANDchildren zillions of times and we always rose to the occasion. The relationships that we developed with Olivia, Carter, and Nolan and every little secret no-no that we had to keep quiet will always be with us. I suppose when all was said and done, the kids spilled all the beans anyway. But we never got fired. Many times the kids have been told that just because you can do thus and so at Grandma's house, doesn't mean you can do it at home. We had rules and we had Grandma's rules—two quite different things.

LOSS OF CLASS

I always thought of myself divided into three parts—worker, mom and wife. All three were always vying for a place in my day. As I look back, long periods of time existed when each had the spotlight. Yet at any given moment, not one of them could be neglected, but someone had to be in the third seat. Perhaps a balance achieved by an intense juggling act is necessary for the successful life women seek. All three factions had to realize their place with me was always secure although the sun might not be shinning on them at the moment.

From the time we first met, Sid always called me George, or, if things were really going well, I was Georgie. Neither of us have any idea how the name came to be. The kids have always called me Mom. I don't recall hearing Mama or Mother. When the girls were little, I used to get really tired of hearing "Mom". Until they got my attention and I said, "Yes", they wouldn't go on with their statement. I must have heard it a hundred times a day when they were little kids.

The kids and marriage had their own chapters. I'm going to talk about Mrs. Corbin here. Teachers, not out of respect, but out of tradition, are known as Mrs. or Mr. Whomever. I was Mrs. Corbin for twenty-seven years.

I became a teacher by default; I wanted to be a businesswoman. Particularly I thought being a buyer for a large department store would be an exciting job. I started out with a business major at Drake University. Then I fell in love, got married and figured out that there weren't any department stores in small town Iowa where I would undoubtedly be living. Instead, I should be a nurse or teacher like most every other female college student back in the early sixties. Since I didn't like the sight of blood, I chose to major in education.

So I was to live out Grandpa Smith's dreaded fear. As I was leaving for Drake in the fall of '60, he was sitting at the kitchen table playing Cribbage with Ray Harbit. He knew I was within earshot when he told Ray, "She'll probably become a teacher or worse yet, marry one." It wasn't that he didn't think teaching was an admirable profession. His point was that there was no money to be made in that career. Financial success was his barometer. How often I heard him chastise some one chiding, "If he's so smart, why ain't he rich." Those who haven't felt riches through enriching others lives would never understand why some of us choose to do what we do.

Then I broke with tradition again and didn't become an elementary teacher. Some people cringed at the thought of teaching high school kids. It worked for me. "Sit down and shut up" flowed out of my mouth quite easily and would probably not be too appropriate for little kids still close to the apron strings.

I really liked teaching. I always got excited in August when it was time to start school again. I never dreaded a Monday morning. I must confess that getting up in the morning any day of the week, however, was never easy. I always watched the end of the Johnny Carson show which was midnight in his early years. Sid helped out in the morning by putting on an LP. It didn't take long for Donna Fargo, singing "I'm the

Happiest Girl in the Whole USA", to make my feet hit the floor. That morning routine sent me off to school for years.

I liked the students; in retrospect, I don't think I ever met a kid I didn't like. They always gave me their best. In fact, it was rare that anyone failed my class. They knew the expectations (academic and behavioral) up front and figured out quickly that they had to meet them. I always told them that nothing would be worse than sitting through my class twice. Not even a handful ever did.

With that first day lecture behind us, we were off and running. Teenage boys aren't particularly interested in reading literature or diagramming sentences, to say nothing of those dreaded essays and term papers. But if you show them "how" to learn, they will. I loathed those teachers that surfaced everywhere over the years telling kids what they needed to know without helping them learn. My motto was, "if they don't learn the way you teach, teach the way they learn." While on the subject, my other pet peeve found among poor teachers was the "gotcha guy". Some rotten teachers pitted themselves against the students and tried to find test questions to stump them. Nasty. Students should be told the content of the test. How else will they know what they need to learn? During that first day lecture, I always told the kids what the questions were on the semester test. It took them eighteen weeks to learn the material, but they knew everything we did the whole semester was heading towards the goal.

I guess my nickname was Sarge and I guess I knew why. I had high demands for myself as a teacher that I passed on to the kids. Roy, the custodian at Lake Mills, always told me when I made the teacher's honor roll on the wall of the boys' restroom. I could usually figure out who the author might have been. I did, however, like teaching boys better than girls. You can tell a guy something once, and that's it. The girls had those darn emotions that got in the way to make teaching more difficult.

And then one day, a kid I didn't have in class called me "bitch"—to my back—as I passed by him in the hall. That was my last year of teaching. The principal said he couldn't do anything about this hallway incident since he couldn't be positive which of three boys standing there was the culprit. So I handled my own discipline of that chap, as usual, and decided maybe I could be more helpful in education on the administrative side of the equation. I thought, "I can do that."

By this time, I had already been to the University of Southern Mississippi to get my Masters Degree. I didn't think much of it at the time, but as I look back, my choice of schools was a bit gutsy—or naïve, depending on your point of view. I enrolled in a two-year summer program offered to three hundred teachers in the States and abroad. We celebrated Eve's graduation from high school one day and I got on an airplane the next day to spend my summer getting smarter. The plane took me to New Orleans where I picked up a taxi and boarded a bus to Hattiesburg. The bus unloaded in front of a K-Mart store that was closed on that Sunday. Eventually, a college official picked me up as scheduled and took me to a dormitory. I found my room crawling with my new roommates. I had never seen a roach before, had never been in the Deep South, had never seen the town or the campus, and didn't know anyone else who had either. I got rid of the roaches, bought a bottle of 409 to scrub the room down and settled in. I found lots of teachers like myself who had left families behind for ten weeks. We muddled through the classes, returned to our classrooms for a year and then finished up the following summer together.

I never forgot students' names in my classes—except over the weekend. I always needed my seating chart every Monday morning. I knew every kid, where he sat, what grade he was getting, the topic of his last essay, a particularly good answer he had given in class discussion, and ad infinitum, but I couldn't recall his/her name after a two day absence. Forty-five years later, I still can bring a face to mind of former students even though the name that goes with it might be missing. But if I hear the name, I can usually remember the person. I taught about 125 students in classes each semester. Over the years, I had the privilege of teaching approximately 7000 different students.

My worst faux pas with student names occurred with a brother and sister in Marion. I don't recall which one came along first. I don't know if the boy was Carl or George and if the girl was Carla or Georgia. Once I messed their names up, I could never get it straight. They were both great kids and anyone could certainly tell which was the boy and which was the girl. I'm sure they never forgave me for not keeping their names straight.

Carrot Bars are part of my legacy from Marion. Fellow teachers requested them when it was my turn for treats. Jars of carrot baby food were even a light-hearted gift from a fellow teacher at Christmas time. My good-cooker friend, Fran Moeller, gave me the recipe. Jon counts *Carrot Bars* among the favorites that arrived with his mother-in-law.

Carrot Bars

4 eggs	2 tsp soda
2 cups sugar	1 cup vegetable oil
1 tsp salt	3 baby food jars carrots
1 tsp cinnamon	2 cups flour

Beat eggs and sugar. Add and mix salt, cinnamon, and soda. Add and mix oil. Add carrots and flour. Beat until smooth. Pour into 10 x 14 greased jellyroll pan. Bake 30 minutes at 350. Cool. Frosting:

1 8 oz softened cream cheese	3 cups powdered sugar
1 stick softened margarine	1 cup chopped walnuts
1 tsp vanilla	

Beat with mixer. Fold in nuts. Frost bars.

* * *

What a thrill it has been to hear about and cross paths with some former students over the years. One of the big advantages of Internet and e-mail is the rekindling and sustaining of acquaintances. Since communication has been made easy, I have connected with some past students. A friend in Indianola told me her daughter had a friend from Iowa State whose hometown was Marion. A note and some catch up with Martha followed. Someone put me in touch with Wendy a few years ago when she was an administrator in Newton. Again, I caught up on news of her twin brother and other siblings and friends. I searched out Ron after hearing that he was a speechwriter for the new Governor Vilsack. When he pleaded guilty to knowing me, I assured him that I would have given him an A had I known he was a Democrat some thirty years earlier in Marion.

Just a few years ago, shortly after I retired, I was doing some consulting in Pella. My small audience, to whom I'm sure I had been introduced as Merry Corbin, consisted of science teachers. Our subject was teaching reading skills in the middle and high school science classroom. An hour or so into the session, I noticed one of the teachers studying me carefully. When I caught his discerning look, he said very cautiously, "Are you **Mrs.** Corbin?" He seemed astonished when I said yes. I told him I didn't know his name but I knew what class he was in at Marion, where he sat, and the girl who became homecoming queen with whom he was good friends. Bob had to supply her name as well as his own.

I've been gratified by students who have looked me up, probably out of sheer curiosity. Sherry, one of my hardworking yearbook editors, took the trouble to search me out twenty years after she graduated. I learned that she was a teacher, a writer, and even developed curriculum for her organization. We still keep in touch.

Near the end of my career, we had dinner with Mike and Georgia, two former students who were high school sweethearts back in the sixties. We sought them out in Des Moines where Mike practices ophthalmology. I was gratified when in our greetings after forty years, Mike said, "You taught me to write." He had graduated from medical school and authored professional books and articles. We had a wonderful evening reminiscing about students from Lake Mills.

Somehow, those students from the first few years of teaching are very vivid in my memory; I can't forget where teaching began for me.

I have to tell one of my favorite "teacher" stories. I was at the blackboard working hard on a grammar lesson involving number and possessives. I had columns drawn on the board and had worked through several examples:

singular	sing. possessive	plural	pl. possessive
dog	*dog's*	*dogs*	*dogs'*
bus	*bus's*	*buses*	*buses'*
candy	*candy's*	*candies*	*candies'*
child	*child's*	*children*	*children's*

The next word was *mouse*. Scott waved his hand profusely so I quickly called on him since he assuredly had the right answer. He proudly announced:

| *mouse* | *mice* | *rat* | *rats* |

Seizing the teaching moment, I asked if he had more than one mouse, would that mean he had rats. He responded with a resounding, two-syllable "ya-a." Today he would have said, "Well, dah." I'm sure I dignified my student's effort and apparent attentiveness to class, even though I couldn't say, "yes" to his answer. (The correct answer, by the way, is mouse, mouse's, mice, mice's.) Some readers might not see this as hilariously funny as I do and might wonder why that teaching moment even sticks in my mind.

Long before I left the classroom, I quit teaching grammar and had to forego diagramming of sentences. I better not get into a conversation of how curriculum content has fallen into the toilet. I can only hope that the old adage, "what goes around, comes around" will apply, dropping grammar back into the classroom. I enjoyed teaching grammar and still delight in giving a lesson to anyone who doesn't know better than to ask for it.

Probably my most famous student to date was Ron Livingston from Marion. I was most proud of him because he graduated from Yale. He and his good buddy, Jason, who went on to become a medical doctor, are great success stories. I always liked Christmas time when they, like lots of other college kids, would visit school.

I had lost track of Ron until one Sunday afternoon in about '95 I was surfing through channels and looked up quickly when I heard a voice that I recognized. It was Ron promoting an upcoming television series. After that I saw him on the big screen starring opposite Jennifer Anniston in *Office Space* and in *Little Black Book*. He was nominated for an Academy Award for Best Supporting Actor in *Band of Brothers*.

I'll take a little bird walk here to say we have an actor in our family. Riley Smith, son of Russ and grandson of Bill and Doris won some good roles in movies. So far, we've seen two, *Radio* and *A New York Minute*, in the theater. He is still in his early twenties so he could have lots more roles ahead of him.

Odds are that many former students have gone on to do great things in a public way. I just haven't heard about them. I spend a lot of time thinking of the whereabouts of students of the past. Undoubtedly, they have made their own families and friends and are productive members of society. I hope they prospered as much from their experiences in the classroom as I did. Eventually, I lost my class, but I'm hoping in a future life we will all meet up again as Sarge's alumni.

As I moved "up" a little ways on the ladder, I wasn't Mrs. Corbin anymore. I became Merry. In retrospect that seems backwards to me, but, I was Merry because I knew if I hoped to accomplish anything as an administrator, then I had to work WITH the teachers. Together we could make a difference and make an impact on thousands of children's lives. Because my license plate said Merry C, some people actually thought the C stood for curriculum. On more than one occasion, a staff number innocently called me Merry Curriculum. I'm sure lots of teachers called me "Sarge", but actually a couple of different superintendents told me to remember whose side I was on. I wanted to say "the kids" but thought better of it.

As a school administrator, like any management person, I made false friends and true enemies. A few folks gave me the time of day just because of my position. Fortunately, however, I count many true friends in Indianola and DeWitt that I have been lucky enough to keep since moving on. Fear of forgetting someone dear to me keeps me from naming names. An exception is Chris who rises above anyone's definition of a true friend. Those who have been "the boss" know that if a decision is rendered eliciting a person's short-comings, a popularity contest is best avoided at the time. I have observed that about a third of a king's subjects don't like anyone who rules—never have and never will. Bosses come to their jobs with true enemies built in and then make a few more on their own,

I became a school administrator due to circumstances out of control. First of all, in 1988 I was fresh out of graduate school with a degree in Curriculum and Instruction. Secondly, the State of Iowa had just passed legislation demanding that all districts document curriculum and instill several mandates into the classroom curriculum. Thirdly, discipline problems and drugs were becoming rampant in the high schools. Legislation and special interest groups were making it difficult to deal with these problems. So with Harold's encouragement, I became involved in efforts to meet the new curriculum criteria in Marion and took classes at Iowa State to become a certified administrator. I officially began my duties in Clinton County with the daunting task of helping three school districts meet the new state curriculum requirements. Four years later I became the Director of Curriculum and Instruction in Indianola.

Teaching was a lot more fun than being an administrator. I never gave up on a kid, but I have to say, that I did give up on some teachers. There were some who are probably still standing in front of the classroom who are never going to be good teachers. In fact, some are bad teachers, but fortunately it is a very small percentage. Education would be greatly improved if the incompetent few could be relocated elsewhere. But unfortunately, the teacher's union has pretty much squelched that and too many administrators have fallen right in with accepting less than mediocrity. I never stumbled onto a teacher who didn't think of him or herself as a great teacher. That's good for the psyche but doesn't say much about what's good for the kids.

Fortunately, a vast majority of teachers are wonderful at their craft and should have a spot in heaven waiting for them. So I moved on with them. Together we brought computers into the buildings and classrooms and taught teachers and students how to use them, switched from a junior high to a middle school and made substantial teaching adjustments that accompanied that movement, intensified the teaching of reading in K-2, taught and learned the latest teaching techniques through staff development opportunities, articulated a curriculum horizontally and vertically in eighteen different subject areas, updated classroom texts and teaching materials, studied and adapted research, measured results, reported on our progress, and a whole lot of other things in hopes of improving what we did for kids in every classroom.

I always remained a teacher but I no longer had class. Instead I had meetings and meetings and meetings—sometimes twenty or twenty-five a week. My greatest thrill was to go to a meeting without scheduling another. It rarely happened. My second biggest joy came if I didn't have to develop the minutes for the meetings. That rarely happened either. I'm relieved that retirement doesn't require a committee.

I was blessed with Boards of Education and Superintendents who let me stick my neck out and teachers who were willing to make major adaptations in their classrooms. Progress in education depends on two things—taking risks and adapting to change. I never shied away from either one at work, at home, or at play.

What was my major role in life? What defines me? Is it my thirty-nine year career in education? Is it sustaining a marriage for over forty-five years? Is it rearing two wonderful daughters and nurturing their children as well? Yes, Yes, and Yes. In the meantime, I've been accused of lots of things. Disorganization was never one of them. I think that's why I was able to hold everything together, if, in fact, I did!

HO HO HO

My life was enriched because I loved my career. I would actually list it as one of my favorite things. Label me "fruitcake" because I also enjoy the holiday season. It always amazed me that a whole bunch of other people don't look forward to the season, and, in fact, dread it. I don't particularly remember liking it as a child, but as an adult, it is my very favorite thing.

Maybe it's my name. For years, I had a vanity license plate on my car that said MERRY C. Strangers would speculate that I was a Christmas baby or that I had a Christmas-related business such as toys or trees or decorations. They always seemed to be disappointed when I told them it was my name. I had fun with that license plate. As cars passed us on the freeway (which didn't happen often), brazen passengers would turn around to see if the front plate was the same as the back plate. It was a chance to smile at a stranger when they acknowledged that it was the same. We enjoyed extra waves and honks on Christmas Day. I always threatened to put a wreath around the front license plate for the holidays. Today, with the bravado of age, I would do it, but the old Iowa license plate now rests in the attic.

I especially like decorating the house for Christmas. We have a picture of our first Christmas tree when we were newlyweds. It was a small tree flocked soft pink. Since we were so proud of our tree, we had Doc Ford come over and take a picture of it. We laugh now at how sparse and ugly it was. The next year we had a bigger tree and it was flocked bright turquoise and had magenta ornaments and no lights. Even it looked better than the first one, as evidenced by the picture that Doc once again trudged through the snow to capture.

I remember the first year we had two trees. It was 1974 in Omaha. We had a formal tree in the living room and a tree the kids decorated in the family room. That year the four of us sat around the kitchen table for hours to make the felt stockings that we stuffed for years. Eve was the little girl, Beth was the angel, Sid was the soldier, and I was Santa Claus. Those stockings haven't been hung for years, but they're still saved in the Christmas barrels in the attic.

We always had REAL trees. They were at the top of my list, right along with REAL fireplaces. But one year in the late nineties we decided to have one real and one artificial tree. I survived. A few years later, we had two artificial trees. I survived again. Sid was delighted not to stand out in the cold holding up several trees, again and again, until I decided which one would best fulfill my Christmas dreams.

Somehow the number of trees continued to increase. I think the maximum occurred in Indianola at the turn of the century. By that time I was really into Christmas decorating. I had large trees in the living room, the family room, the game room, and our bedroom, and smaller trees tucked into other strategic places. I wasn't counting until Scott, a neighbor, once remarked that he was appalled that we had seven trees. Surprised, I said, "We do?" Thinking he was exaggerating, I counted, and he had missed one.

Eventually, the trees were no longer the focus of the decorating. I had Christmas stuff everywhere. The joke was, if you stood still for more than a few minutes, you were likely to end up with a bow or a sprig of evergreen adorning your body. Actually, all these years I was collecting some beautiful pieces for Christmas that I hope remain with our family for generations. I am particularly fond of two snowflake woolen stockings from Austria, the beautiful painted Santa face complete with red velvet hat made by artisan Helen Lindenmuth, the skaters from Roesle's St. Nicholas Collection, the nativity scene gathered piece by piece, the Lenox Christmas China with dinner plates representing each of the thirteen original colonies, and the Holly and Ivy Irish stoneware.

In the eighties we started to collect Christmas tree ornaments as souvenirs of our travels. We are still gathering them since they are usually readily available, small to transport, and an excuse to seek out Christmas shops. We especially enjoy the nostalgia associated with traveling as we place each one on the tree. That same tree also holds all the ornaments, several hand made, from friends over the years. We round out the tree with the ornaments that Beth and Eve chose as little girls when they had complained loud enough about "Mom's" tree to secure one of their own.

At about the same time, I began giving the girls a dated Hallmark ornament each year. One year as teen-agers, they didn't bother to unwrap the particular gift detected as the "dumb ole ornament". That ended the tradition, but I have noticed that a dozen or so still hang on their trees in their homes.

Baking the goodies at Christmas time pre-dominated a large share of the holiday preparation time. I used to bake dozens of different cookies and candies after spending the year searching out new recipes. Since cream, butter, and sugar aren't much in favor anymore, I have cut back on the baking. Two of our favorites that will always rest in the tins on the counter are Cashew Cookies and Sid's fudge. The cashew cookies were from Doris, the girls' marvelous baby sitter when they were preschool age. One of Sid's co-workers at Smulekoff's shared her fudge recipe.

Cashew Cookies

1/2 cup margarine

1 cup packed brown sugar

1 egg

1/4 tsp vanilla

2 cups flour

3/4 tsp soda

3/4 tsp baking powder

1/3 cup dairy sour cream

1 1/2 cups salted cashew pieces

Cream margarine and sugar until light and fluffy. Beat in egg and vanilla. Add sifted dry ingredients alternately with sour cream and mix well. Fold in cashews. Drop by teaspoonful on a greased cookie sheet. Bake at 375 for 8 minutes until lightly browned. Cool and frost:

1/2 cup margarine

3 T cream

3/4 tsp vanilla

2 cups powdered sugar

Lightly brown the butter. Remove from heat. Add cream and vanilla. Stir in powdered sugar. Mix until smooth and put on cookies. Recipe makes a small batch of cookies but can be doubled.

* * *

Fudge

4 1/2 cups white sugar	24 oz bag chocolate chips
1 large can evaporated milk	3 T vanilla
1/2 pound butter	2 cups chopped nuts

Heat sugar and milk, stirring constantly until reaching a rolling boil. Cook 6 minutes while continuing to stir. Remove from heat. Add butter, chocolate chips and vanilla. Stir until chips are melted. Add nuts. Stir until thick enough to pour into 9 x 13 inch pan. Put in refrigerator until set. Cut into pieces. Store in refrigerator but serve at room temperature.

*   *   *

Christmas Cards are close to the top of my list of favorite Christmas traditions. I eagerly await greetings from people who were in our lives many years ago, but, unfortunately, are only heard from at the holidays. When we first moved from a community, we would keep up for a few years and then one by one, they dropped off the list. I regret that. From my standpoint, I never dreaded writing the Christmas cards either. I have kept a copy of each card with the accompanying letter that I sent each year since the early sixties. I suppose someone will toss that scrapbook some day, but it has turned out to be a chronicle of our family that helps us reminisce each season.

And probably most of all, I enjoy entertaining family at Christmas. We had many family Christmases at our house, sharing Christmas Eve with McTaggarts and Terry's family while the kids were growing up. Christmas Day venues fluctuated but each remains special. With grandchildren on the scene, we now share the holidays with our immediate family.

Green Bean Casserole always appears on our holiday table. We usually make a double batch and Beth makes a triple batch to avoid Jon and Eve plotting to get the leftovers. In the late sixties we were visiting the Phelps family in Indianola and they served this recipe from their friends, the Stovers. Thirty years later, we moved to Indianola and met up with Max and Virginia again. I mentioned that the vegetable still graces our holiday table and Virginia said it is one of their family's favorite holiday foods as well.

Green Bean Casserole

2 T melted butter	1 cup dairy sour cream
2 T flour	2 cans green beans, drained
1 tsp salt	6 ozs grated Swiss cheese
1/4 tsp pepper	2 cups crushed corn flakes
1/2 tsp grated onion	2 T melted butter

Mix first 5 ingredients and stir in sour cream. Add drained beans. Layer beans and cheese twice in 1 1/2 quart casserole. Top with corn flakes mixed with butter. Bake 20 minutes at 400.

*   *   *

By the end of the seventies I had branded my own concoction for stuffing, which Beth dubbed *Mom's Dressing*, to accompany the holiday turkey. I eventually wrote it down for those who asked for it, but cooks have to feel their way through the additions, particularly the amount of moisture. It starts with Kellogg's Stuffing mix. Eventually the packaging and then the availability of the mix changed. Jon couldn't find the mix in Milwaukee last Christmas so he had his mother ship four boxes to him so that I would be able to get the real thing stirred up for the usual feast.

Mom's Dressing

3 pkgs herb seasoned stuffing mix	2 cans mushroom soup
1/2–1 cup turkey	1 can celery soup
5 cups salted water	2 tsp sage
1/2 lb butter	2 tsp poultry seasoning
2 cups chopped celery	1 tsp pepper
1 cup chopped onion	4 cups hot turkey broth
2 medium apples, peeled, chopped	1 can chicken broth

Boil turkey neck in 5 cups of water until cooked. Remove turkey from bones. Reserve the broth. Saute celery and onion in butter. Add to stuffing mix and turkey. Add apples, undiluted soups, and spices. Pour hot turkey broth over all. Mix well allowing stuffing to absorb liquid. Add canned chicken broth and/or hot water to make the consistency desired. Bake 90 minutes at 350 in roaster sprayed with Pam. Sliced mushrooms and chopped walnuts can be added for variation.

* * *

Santa actually arrived at Grandma's house when Nolan was a little tike and was still coming around when Olivia could crawl upon his lap. Bob Klinge, a top class teacher, who displays more optimism daily than most people ever muster up, would ring the doorbell and surprise everyone with his HO, HO, HO. The fun of choosing children's presents and seeing their happiness is one of my greatest treasures. But some years, there were no kids so Sid and I did our own thing. Our favorite was Christmas at the Opryland Hotel in Nashville where even Ebenezer Scrooge would get into the holiday spirit. I've never quite gotten past the fact that just because Eve and Beth got married, my favorite tradition of Christmas Eve ended, but it did.

A party or two given for friends was always part of the season's celebration. Included were brunches, lunches, dinners, cocktail parties, lady's bridge, dinner bridge, club hosting, and co-worker parties. Whatever the reason, we loved Christmas festivities at our house. The largest was the Christmas House Walk when over 700 people signed the guest book on the annual fund-raising house tour in Indianola.

One brunch recipe that I've served repeatedly—not just at Christmas—is usually met with recipe requests. I cut it out of a newspaper featuring dishes from Iowa country clubs a couple of decades ago.

Favorite Brunch Casserole

1/4 cup butter	9 slices sharp processed cheese
1/2 lb sliced fresh mushrooms	4 large eggs, well beaten
9 slices bread	2 cups milk
4 cups diced cooked chicken	1 tsp salt
1 8 oz can sliced water chestnuts	1 can mushroom soup
4 oz pkg slivered almonds	1 can celery soup
3/4 cup stuffed sliced olives	buttered bread crumbs

Melt butter in saucepan. Saute mushrooms in butter 4 minutes. Remove crusts from bread slices. Line shallow buttered 9 x 13 dish with bread slices. Top with chicken. Follow with layers of mushrooms, water chestnuts, olive slices, and slivered almond. Top with cheese. Combine eggs, milk and salt in small bowl. Pour over cheese. Combine soups, undiluted; spread on top. Cover with foil and refrigerate overnight. Bake covered at 350 for 45 minutes. Sprinkle with buttered bread crumbs and bake 15 minutes longer uncovered. Let set 15 minutes before cutting into serving pieces. Serves 9-12.

*   *   *

We love visiting the festive homes of friends and family. Christmas wouldn't be complete with out the holiday open houses and a chance to visit others whose friendships we value all year long. Fran Moeller was the all time great party hostess in Le Mars anytime of the year. Her house was always filled with cheer. I remember the deviled egg we found in the greenery on the open stairway banister in the wee hours of the morning following her Christmas party. For months, bent over the one proverbial beer, we speculated who would have stuck it there.

My deviled egg recipe developed over several years. I often served them at parties because they disappeared so fast. The secret is good homemade pickle relish. Sid's Mom and Aunt Laurie supplied it for years from vegetables in their gardens; now I have it shipped by the case from Bea's in Door County. This recipe (like the potato salad) depends on the relish.

Deviled Eggs

9 hard boiled eggs	3 T pickle relish
4 T mayonnaise	1/4 tsp salt
1 1/2 tsp mustard	1/8 tsp pepper
1 tsp lemon juice	dash of Accent

Peel eggs, cut in half lengthwise and remove yolks. Mash yolks and add above ingredients. Mix well. Stuff mixture back into egg halves. Garnish with paprika or herbs.

*   *   *

Missy Chrissy is another best friend who also rates best cook and best hostess. I don't have any of Chris's recipes because she doesn't use recipes, and on the rare occasion that she does, she alters them anyway. Chris can imagine any excuse to throw a party—Christmas and Cinco de Mayo are regulars—and keeps everyone whooping it up for hours.

In the wee small hours of the morning at one of her parties, she got out the dog clippers. Santa was there, too, witnessing the shearing. Sid was totally bald on top of his head from that day forward.

A FEW OF MY FAVORITE THINGS

Coming in second place right behind Christmas on my list of favorites would be throwing a party. Sid and I love to entertain guests, drop in or invited. People think we are a bit zappy, but much of the preparation we actually enjoy, like cleaning, cooking, planning, and decorating. And then we get to eat, drink, and be merry. What's not to like?

Over the years we have entertained lots of overnight guests and always hoped each would return. Dick Polansky composed the following poem early one morning on our front porch in Indianola during a weekend of fun. Though flattering to us, it really demonstrates the creativity and thoughtfulness that we cherish in his friendship.

SID & MERRY'S PLACE

This world of ours may ne're define
the nature of a host
from out a gloomy world sublime
with things we fear the most.

Each mortal man should then aspire
to what the gods would seek,
and try to set his world on fire
or save the mild and meek.

So in this course of world events
I knew that I would find
a couple bent on sealing rents
among the social blind.

For they do more than entertain
within a common place.
They'll siphon off your daily pain
with elegance and grace.

You're made to feel so welcome
at Sid and Merry's place.
In time you'll find you could succumb
to life styled at their pace.

So be prepared for Iowa charm,
more fine than Belgium lace.
They'll pop a cork, scrape off the barm,
or open up a case.

> *When you are forced to leave their home*
> *you'll wear a happy face,*
> *and bid farewell, good-by, shalom*
> *to Sid and Merry's place!*

Friends might expect me to say that cooking is one of my favorite things. But the truth of the matter is that I enjoy eating; this book won't be long enough to list my favorite foods. In another life I might write a cookbook or a newspaper column sharing my favorite recipes. However, I don't think I could cope with the irritation of people altering my recipes. I follow recipes to the last pinch of salt and always hassle my creative friends who don't.

If you have had dinner at our house in the past twenty-five years, I've probably served you *Baked Chicken Breast*. Kim, my first yearbook editor, gave me the recipe. Eve and Beth have both served it to most of their first-time guests (or second-time, since Eve says it's what she always serves). The good part about moving to new places is that I have new guests so I can repeat it. It's a good choice, just like grabbing your favorite old sweater out of the closet for comfort on a cool fall day.

Baked Chicken Breast

1 3-4 oz pkg dried beef	8 oz dairy sour cream
4 strips bacon	4 boned/skinned chicken breast halves
1 can mushroom soup	

Line bottom and sides of baking dish with dried beef. Wrap one strip of bacon around each chicken breast. Place in dish and cover with mixture of soup and sour cream. Bake uncovered for 3 hours at 275. (Chicken breasts/bacon can be added without increasing the sauce.)

*   *   *

My quest for recipes and cooking talent grew to new heights as our dinner duplicate bridge group in Le Mars turned into a gourmet club with a long cocktail hour for starters and bridge as the after thought. Harkers, Dulls, Knudtsons, and Juons were partners in culinary crime from the beginning. When we moved, Jack flew the five other couples to Omaha when it was our yearly turn to host. The Galloping Gourmet had nothing on us. Knudtsons moved to Cedar Rapids shortly before we did. The four of us didn't waste any time rounding up four other couples for a new group which we were part of for nearly twenty years. We dined, played bridge, and scored at the bottom behind Klopfensteins and Fishels, all with unrelenting consistency.

We always tucked a tossed salad in between the appetizer and the main course. I don't know where either of these recipes came from—probably magazines—but I've passed both recipes on umpteen times in the past twenty-five years.

Strawberry-Spinach Salad

1 bag fresh spinach	1 1/2 tsp minced onion
1 pint fresh strawberries	1/4 tsp paprika
1/2 cup sugar	1/2 cup vegetable oil
2 T sesame seed	1/4 cup cider vinegar
1 T poppy seed	

Arrange spinach and berries in bowl or on salad plates. Place next 5 ingredients in blender. With blender running, add oil and vinegar in a slow, steady stream until thoroughly mixed and thickened (about 1 minute). Drizzle over spinach. Serve immediately.

* * *

Mandarin Orange Tossed Salad

1/4 cup sliced almonds	1 cup chopped celery
1 T + 1 tsp sugar	3 green onions, sliced thin
1/2 head iceberg	1 11oz can mandarin oranges, drained
1/4 head romaine	

Make dressing. Cook and stir almonds and sugar in skillet over low heat until sugar melts and almonds are coated. Cool, break apart and reserve. Tear lettuces into bite-size pieces and put in plastic bag; add celery and onions. Close securely and refrigerate. Pour dressing into bag 5 minutes before serving; add oranges. Fasten bag securely; shake until greens are well coated. Add almonds and shake. Dressing:

1/4 cup vegetable oil	1 T snipped parsley
2 T vinegar	½ tsp salt; dash pepper
2 T sugar	dash red pepper sauce

Shake all ingredients in tightly covered jar. Refrigerate at least 1 hour.

*   *   *

I must share our favorite cocktail desserts for entertaining. Since I couldn't choose between them, both are included. *Pink Squirrels* and *Nutty Monks* are refreshing following any meal and especially when the conversation moves to the patio after dinner.

Pink Squirrels

4 scoops vanilla ice cream   2 oz cream de cacao

2 oz cream de almond

Blend ingredients in a blender or with a mixer. Serve immediately in stemmed cocktail glasses.

*   *   *

Nutty Monks

4 scoops French vanilla ice cream   2 oz cream de cacao

2 oz Frangelica   1 crushed Butterfinger candy bar

Blend ingredients in a blender. Serve immediately in stemmed cocktail glasses.

*   *   *

I would be remiss if I moved on from a discussion of my favorite things without mentioning dishes. I can't get past a department store or antique shop without checking out the breakables. A platter or bowl will draw my attention quicker than any other pretty piece of art.

This passion goes back to my childhood. My cedar chest held my mom's "everyday" dishes that were used on the table in the early years of our marriage. The antique stores are full of the green glass Fire King (made in the USA) dishes that came as gifts from the grocery store back in the forties. The plates always reminded me of a pie because of the crimped edges.

When I was about twelve, Grandma Otterbeck gave each of her six grandchildren a chance to pick something from her home to keep as a memory of her. I chose her Noritake china, a set of twelve of the

Sheridan pattern. We started our marriage with the beautiful china and the silver flatware Grandma gave us as a wedding gift.

In the late sixties in Le Mars we occasionally went to auctions on the weekend. I couldn't resist bidding on two baskets of china that sold really cheap. I got them home and discovered that I had twelve place settings of Noritake dishes, the Azalea pattern. The set had an abundance of serving pieces in excellent condition.

My suspicion on both of my sets of dishes was that soldiers and seamen had brought the Noritake back from war duty in Japan. Not so. The china had come piece by piece with soap coupons. Grandma Otterbeck had obtained hers that way. I've always wondered how many boxes of soap and how many years it must have taken to complete the sets.

When Beth and Eve were teen-agers, I asked them to choose which set they would someday like. Beth chose the Sheridan because it was a family heirloom. Eve chose the Azalea because she liked pink. They were each given the china as a wedding gift. Both of them use the china regularly in their homes. Ironically, the respective patterns fit their decors perfectly.

The story doesn't stop there. I discovered that the two sets are the number 1 and number 2 antique china patterns collected. About the time of this discovery, EBAY was getting started which gave me a new hobby searching and bidding on my passion, dishes. I would get up in the middle of the night to try to outsmart other bidders. I landed lots of pieces (and several escaped). Dave picked up on my passion once he figured out the monetary value of the collection. He still studies and purchases the unique pieces that accompany the Azalea pattern.

Well, once my china was gone I had to choose a new pattern. Darn. My collecting went from there until I won't admit how many sets I have. As with any good chip off the old block, Beth isn't far behind me. Eve pointed out on her last visit to Texas that my pantry contained way more dishes than food. And what's the matter with that?

Grandma Smith taught me a couple of tricks about cooking. When we would hurry into the house a bit late for a meal, we would immediately set the table first. If Grandpa showed up in the kitchen, it would look like the meal was under control. Grandma's special salad recipe in her handwriting is a cherished family heirloom.

24 Hour Salad

1 large can pineapple chunks	2 cups miniature marshmallows
1 cup pineapple juice	1 cup walnut or pecan pieces
2 eggs beaten	1 lb seedless red grapes
4 T flour	2 bananas
1 cup sugar	

Drain pineapple and add water to reserved juice to equal 1 cup. Cook eggs, pineapple juice, flour, sugar and salt stirring constantly until thickened. Cool. Add to marshmallows, grapes, pineapple and nuts. Refrigerate overnight. Mix in bananas before serving.

*   *   *

Grandma also stressed the importance of getting out the pretty china. There was no need to wait for a special occasion since every meal was important. Her request was honored to give each of her grand and great grand children a piece of her Johnson Bros. English porcelain that had been given to her by her family. I never fail to look for more pieces in antique stores, but to no avail. The hunt would be a great excuse for an adventure to England again.

My favorite books and authors are from England, as well. My list would start with Shakespeare and the early British novels of the eighteenth century. I never could satisfy my reading appetite for the Brontes, Fielding, DeFoe, Jane Austin and Virginia Wolfe, to mention a few. *Jane Eyre* is probably my all time favorite book. My favorite movie is *The Hours*, a wonderfully complicated story of three women living in different eras with lives connected by Virginia Wolfe's novel, *Mrs. Dalloway*. An earlier movie *Who's Afraid of Virginia Wolfe* starring my favorite actress, Elizabeth Taylor, sticks with me also.

The past few years I have preferred reading nonfiction, particularly autobiography, trashy novels, and one romantic author, Robert James Waller. I have every one of Waller's books since devouring *Bridges of Madison County*. The setting is in the county just down the road from Indianola. We watched the filming of the movie in Winterset one Sunday afternoon but unfortunately didn't catch a glimpse of Meryl Streep or Clint Eastwood, two more of my favorites. I can't leave out poetry as a preferred literature. Robert Frost, Emily Dickinson, and e.e. cummings are particular favorites, but any poet is a treat.

I guess most anything British is pretty high on my list. The Cotswolds in England is the most favorite place I have ever visited. It's idyllic landscape and stone villages provide a mellow and serene atmosphere as if to say, "Sit and stay awhile." When approached with the conversation starter, what might you have done differently in your life, my first answer would be, develop a British accent.

Also, I would have more kids. I think I did that easily and I'm sure I did it well. The proof is in the pudding. About the only other thing I would change in my life if given the chance to live it again would be to become a singer. I love singing along with the radio in the car, but just once I would like to take the stage and belt out a beauty to thousands of people. Oh, yes, I would like to be an artist, too, but I could save that for another life.

I believe in reincarnation. This life was my concrete sequential life with all the organizational skills I could muster up, but when I come around again, I'm going to bolster my creativity. Then my friend Edie can't call me anal because of my affinity for neatness and organization.

I'm not a very religious person, but I do believe in God, heaven, and the power of prayer. My belief in heaven helps me deal with death. I'm comforted knowing where the people are that have left already and where the rest of you are going. I know prayer works because the planes I've been on never crashed.

But I'm supposed to be discussing my favorite things. I'm not sure anyone would call "hair" a favorite thing, but it is a very IMPORTANT thing to me. Hair is the first thing I notice about any one. Ask me to describe someone and I begin with their hair. I guess I have a hair fettish, or it may be that I styled hair in one of my former lives. Or maybe I'm gearing up for reincarnation.

The girls' hair was always important to me while they were growing up. They always had the benefit of a good hair stylist. Jon let me in on a little secret. To this day, he claims Beth schedules a hair cut and highlight when we are going to be seeing each other. I guess I've given her a complex—more than one, she would add. Neither of the girls is satisfied with their own hair because they think they have too much curl. It came from the Otterbeck gene pool.

I used to be crazy about hats, especially the Hedda Hopper type. They range from fake leopard to real mink and every fabric and color in between. My favorite is made from a peach-colored chiffon scarf (at least twenty feet long) wrapped round and round to form a huge beehive. The tail of the scarf hangs down about four feet to wrap around the neck. No, I'm not kidding, and yes, I actually wore it—several times. Since the early sixties, this style of hat has not been in vogue, but, trust me here, it once was. As we moved from house to house, the hats were stacked on top of each other in the new attic. I would be hard pressed to find an excuse for hoarding hats, but I haven't yet been held accountable for this weakness. Some day I'm going to plop my chartreuse hat with the big floppy brim smack dab on top of my head and show up at the Kentucky Derby.

I also like to gamble. The morning after my last day of work, we hopped on a plane headed for New Orleans to spend two weeks on the Gulf Shore gambling in the casinos that Hurricane Katrina destroyed a couple of years later. That was truly a dream vacation, my response to Sid's invitation to choose a spot to celebrate my retirement.

I have a bunch of other favorites. Color is one of them. I like the color purple. I also think the classiest color is black. Actually, there isn't any color I don't like. Every color has its place and time if used in harmony with the other colors around it. When my mind is in neutral, the names of colors race through it. Some people hum tunes, some people think numbers, but I recite colors. When it comes to colors of metal, silver (make mine white gold) is my favorite. Silver goes best with diamonds, another favorite. My list could go on, but I said I would share a FEW of my favorite things.

JUST FOR THE FUN OF IT

I've gotten in plenty of trouble throughout my life, all in the name of fun. I never did regret that too much, but I have to say that now I'm really glad I took advantage of so many fun things that presented themselves along the way. When looking for the thread that held our lives together, it was probably music, music, music in one form or another.

We could have danced all night,
we could have danced all night,
and still come back for more.

Sid and I danced on our first date. The band was probably Leo Greco or Andy Doll, I don't remember for sure. But I do remember getting my first dance instruction. It was complete with Sid counting the beat in my ear. His entertainment was ballroom dances all through college. He probably was considered a good catch at the dances since available guys were greatly outnumbered by single women.

I jitterbugged to our 45-rpm records in Ford's basement and watched American Bandstand after school in their living room long before Sid came along. To be a teen-ager in the fifties, you had to jitterbug. I had a small portable record player complete with the plastic spindle to hold a stack of 45-rpm records. I bought them as often as I could for under a buck apiece. One side was the hit and the other side was a pretty trashy second-rate song. I can still hear each record drop as we waited to see if we could sit through the song or if we just had to get up and dance. There wasn't a song in the fifties that wasn't made for dancing.

Sid and I danced every weekend. We would either go to a dance hall in the area or a nightclub for dinner and dancing. There was usually a band at *Pine Lodge* or the *Sportsman* in Oelwein. Our favorite nightclub, though, was *Blue Heaven* in Prairie du Chien, Wisconsin. On Sunday trips to Prairie, we would frequent a dirt-floored dive called *Spit an' Whistle*, or we could dance on Sunday afternoons at *Ambrose Park*. Risking the law by taking a minor across a state line and buying her booze evidently never occurred to Sid.

Nightclubs as we knew them have disappeared. Today they are Supper Clubs, Dinner Clubs, Fine Dining, or you name it. One of the distinctive things of yesteryear's nightclub was the hors d'oeuvres tray (or horses' ovaries as Doc used to call them). As soon as diners were seated and the drink orders were taken, the waitress delivered the relishes to the center of the table. We never had to ask for them and no charge ever occurred on the bill. On the big round tray, which sometimes spun around, you could choose from vegetables, dips, cheese, crackers, Braunschweiger, liver pate or some other spiced-up meat. I never thought I would mourn the loss of a wilted celery stick, but I do. Those WERE the good ole days.

Another sad disappearing act came with the closing of Bishop's cafeteria. Sid and I ate our very first meal together at Bishop's in Waterloo at the Northeast Iowa Band Festival. We still enjoyed the favorite place at Lindale Plaza in Cedar Rapids when the girls were teen-agers. The long row of food choices provided something for every palette. It was so attractively presented and tasted good besides. We carefully chose each entrée as if with great thought, although each of us usually repeated time after time. How important we felt when a lady dressed in a starched, gray uniform complete with a crisp white hat (like those that distinguished a registered nurse) carried the tray to the table selected just for us. And in case we passed up Coconut Cream Pie but still had room for it, a battery-operated candle sat on each table to signal help from the waitress. The tables were dressed in white cloths and the chairs were wonderfully upholstered barrel and wingback chairs on castors. It didn't get much better than dinner at Bishop's. They were way ahead of their time and never could be confused with the cheap, all-you-can-stuff places today.

The late fifties and early sixties made up the Big Band era. We danced to most of them. Other times we clung to our seats and shuffled our feet while we watched the bands in concert. Guy Lombardo, Louis Armstrong, Tommy and Jimmy Dorsey, Benny Goodman, Lawrence Welk, Wayne King, and Glenn Miller all made their rounds in Iowa.

Ballroom dancing fell out of favor in the seventies causing most of the dance halls to close. For a couple of decades we were pretty much confined to dancing at wedding receptions and special occasions like the few Saturday nights we could break away from raising the kids.

Retirement has connected us with people our age, Texas bars, dance halls that had never closed, and time to do what we love most. And thanks to *Dancing with the Stars* and other reality television shows, dancing is popular once again.

For as much as we both loved to cook and entertain, we sure ate out a lot. I always joked that Sid would have a tough time deciding whether it was eating or dancing that he enjoyed most. Actually, he probably would have put something else at the top of his list.

Our travels have always focused on food. Where and what are we going to eat were the questions for the day. We have dined in five-star restaurants and others that we would rate that high. I can't begin to remember the names of even a few of them, but we both remember hundreds of dining experiences because of the restaurant, the food, the setting, or the dining partners.

We had a three-hour dining experience with Tom and Kari at the Wild Boar in Nashville. That's the only time we experienced each of us having our own waiter serving in unison when the conversation paused briefly to allow them to proceed. The delicacy in Malta was grilled rabbit. We chose a top-notch restaurant in an old horse stable and dined in our private horse stall. On that vacation, we also took an hour-long ferry trip to Gozo, a smaller Maltese Island. We had lunch seaside on the patio of a restaurant owned by a fisherman and his wife. We picked out the whole fish we wanted from those waiting patiently (without choice) on a bed of ice. Once cooked, the fisherman's wife presented it to us on a large tray. She then proceeded to carve it. The head, tail, innards and skeleton ended up in her bucket. She then placed the delicious fish—a native kind we had not heard of—on our plates and we savored every morsel.

Ebbitt's Grill in Washington DC has a gorgeous dining room. A visit to the ladies room where fresh warm linen towels awaited was the epitome of elegance. On San Francisco, the elevator ride to the Empress of China, known then as the Chinese restaurant of the stars, gave us a chance to see the autographs of many famous people. I searched for a pen to leave my signature. Sid was glad when I couldn't come up with one.

We have experienced dinners in restaurants where both the waiter and menu were in a language foreign to us. One particular elegant place was a French restaurant in Quebec. We still don't know what we savored; we may have said no thanks if we knew its source. We did know what we weren't eating when Mike Saunders ordered grossly bloated duck livers more appetizingly known as Fois Gras at Las Canarias in San Antonio.

My list could go on for pages, but I'll stop after a plug for Baltimore where we experienced abundant and wonderful seafood restaurants. No, I probably should say San Francisco for its ethnic food variety. I would be remiss if I didn't mention the excellent places that the kids, knowing our love for dining experiences, have taken us to in Kansas City and Milwaukee. Eve arranged for us to return to Idaho Springs, Colorado, on a recent ski trip to savor the Mountain Pies that she and Beth remembered from their childhood.

Searching out the good restaurants wherever we lived was always a weekend event. We spent many memorable Saturday nights visiting restaurants throughout the southeastern edge of Iowa with Randy and Nancy. No dive that a patient of Randy's may have mentioned escaped us. I particularly remember a place back in a field near the Mississippi River. When Nancy placed her order, she was told, "We ain't got no wine." The steaks, which Randy had promoted as the draw, came on paper plates with a basket of white Colonial sandwich bread. We loved the place stuffed with people from tarpaper wall to tarpaper wall.

Both Sid and I grew up enjoying the catch from the fisherman in our families. Fried catfish and crappies served with fried potatoes was a treat. Sid did a little fishing at our cottage on Rice Lake, but that didn't satisfy our taste buds. What we really liked was Friday night fish fries. We missed them in Central Iowa, but always looked forward to them in Eastern Iowa and at Beth's in Milwaukee. We were pleasantly surprised to find catfish fries everywhere in hot, dry Texas.

But I digressed again. I was talking about the fun that music brought to our lives through dancing. Another great music venue for us was Broadway musicals, most of which we saw when they were on tour. Our very first one was *South Pacific* staring Mary Martin. We lived in Lake Mills at the time and drove to Des Moines with Harry and Linda for the experience at the KRNT Theater. We were hooked. Later years we saw Cloris Leachman in *Showboat*, and John Davidson in *State Fair*. Most of the others had Broadway players, not as well known to us.

I swooned over John Davidson in the seventies. He had temporarily replaced Elvis as my idol. This particular evening John was on television. I was sitting Indian style dressed in a long velour robe that Sid had given me for Christmas. I became so engrossed that I didn't notice my hand holding a burning cigarette had dropped into my lap.

When I stood up, burn holes dotted the front of my robe. While I'm talking about myself and robes, I should add Val Moeller's favorite story—at least it was the biggest laugh I ever heard from him. One morning dressed in a robe and apparently little else, I leaned across the breakfast table and dropped a boob in my oatmeal bowl. Messy.

We have seen many of the major musicals of the past forty years and probably never met one we didn't like. I still get goose bumps when I think about seeing *Les Miserables* from our front row seats in the balcony of the Kennedy Center in Washington DC. Where better to see *Lion King* performed by the original cast than in London in the Lyceum Theater with Jacquie and Carroll on our British Isles trip.

My pick of musicals, though, is *Cats* on which my favorite composer, Andrew Lloyd Webber, out did himself. The outstanding music and beautifully costumed cats dancing around the stage were breathtaking. *Evita* and *Jesus Christ Super Star* are my other favorite Weber shows. I could sit through any of his musicals several times. When Sid wanted to see favorite productions a second time, I always said no because there were too many things to see for the first time. He would have chosen to see *Phantom of the Opera* a third time.

When it comes to music, I have to give a little space to Opera. Dick Polansky deserves the credit for acquainting us with Opera and for encouraging us to attend. We had one of the best theaters and the Des Moines Opera Company performing near our own backyard in Indianola. We learned to appreciate the beauty of opera and eagerly awaited the performances every summer.

When we had a chance and a nickel in our pocket we would get tickets for live performances that were close by. My most cherished, of course, was Elvis. I was thirty something by the time we saw him in Omaha on his comeback tour not long before his death. I'm not sure I breathed through the whole thing, but I did gasp when his bodyguards shoved their boots into the faces of women trying to climb onto the stage. It was not a pretty sight.

When we were at Holiday Island visiting Bill and Doris, we went to see Anita Bryant. Bill already had the tickets close to the stage and set apart from the rest of the audience. I hadn't caught on that this was another one of Bill's set-ups. When Anita came to a place in the performance where she wanted volunteers to rock and roll with her, she headed right for Sid. He was a willing partner. After dancing to a ditty in her routine, she asked her band to start over because this partner could really dance. The band obliged.

The neat thing about Las Vegas is that a whole bunch of stars gather there so you can catch several acts in a few days. My trip to Vegas with Judy was especially memorable. Judy and I taught together in Le Mars where she was widowed with two small children. She asked me to go on vacation with her so we chose Vegas. The details of the trip have always remained top secret but suffice it to say, we laughed for five days straight. In between, we saw performances by Paul Anka, Sammy Davis Jr., Gladys Knight and the Pips, Patty Page, and Wayne Newton.

On multiple trips to Branson and Nashville we've enjoyed the country music stars. We appreciate their music and dance to it more than any other type now that we are in Texas. We've been to the Grand Ole Opry several times where you can catch at least ten country stars on a Saturday night. We saw Minnie Pearl and "Stand By Your Man" Tammy Wynette, Porter Wagner, and Bill Anderson, to name a few. Martina McBride, Barbara Mandrell, Oak Ridge Boys, Clint Black, Wynona Judd, Brooks and Dunn, and Billy Ray Cyrus gave unforgettable performances at various venues.

We saw Brenda Lee at the Gala ballroom in Independence in the early sixties. She wasn't much bigger than a minute. Sid's thrill was hearing Boots Randolph play *Yackety Sax* early one morning in South Dakota. We used to go out into the county after the bars closed in Sioux Falls on our Saturday night outings in the early seventies with Nick and Dolores. Also, way back when, Helen Reddy and John Denver put on terrific shows. The Christy Minstrels recorded our all time favorite Christmas album. They toured in Iowa in the sixties and were exceptional, but they were probably too big of a group to stay together for very long. Andy Williams and Roger Williams also come to mind from a bunch of decades ago. Our LP vinyl records have been saved;

hopefully someday the kids will enjoy listening to the music of by-gone eras.

 I spotted Vince Gill at the Des Moines Country Club where we were having a meeting; he was playing golf while in town for the State Fair. When I asked for his autograph, he stuck his golf sock in his mouth to free his hand and oblige my request. Later, our group played golf, and as luck would have it, Vince came in from his round and I got his cart. Needless to say, I chose to sit in the spot he had just vacated.

 My other claim-to-fame sightings are of Queen Elizabeth and Prince Phillip getting into their chauffer-driven car at Windsor Castle, Roseanne Barr with her husband Tom Arnold ducking out early from an Iowa Football game, and George and Barbara Bush at his library in College Station. Lute Olson caught me off guard while walking down the street in Iowa City. Speaking first, he said, "Sure warm, isn't it." Without thinking I said, "Hotter than Hell", which it was in July in Iowa. Everyone has "I saw So-n-So" stories; it always amazed me that no one else really cares.

 I've rattled on about all this fun we have had in our lives and haven't mentioned Beth (Ford) and Rob Hampel. They have been our friends for life. Beth and I grew up together in Lamont, we all four graduated from the same college, and we both lived in Cedar Rapids/Marion for years so a majority of our memorable events were with them. We've snow skied, boated, watched Iowa football games, played bridge, wined and dined, shopped, celebrated holidays, and just sat and talked an infinite number of times. Whenever there was something new and exciting to do, we often experienced it together. Sid and Rob can't even estimate the number of beers they've downed together—but thousands would be conservative. The basis of our friendship is laughter—not recalling a time when we didn't have fun. Both Rob and Sid are nuttier than fruitcakes causing us all to laugh at each other.

 Speaking of nuts and Rob, on a recent visit I served he and Beth a new cake recipe that Jacquie gave me. It was delicious but lacked a suitable name—one that lived up to the cake's unique characteristics.

Rob named them *Cajones*. I hesitate to include a recipe that isn't an oldie but it really is a goody.

Cajones

1 box white cake mix	12 oz white almond bark coating
3/4 can white frosting	12 oz white chocolate chips

Bake cake as directed. Cool. Crumble cake into small pieces. Mix frosting into cake crumbs. Scoop 1 tablespoon of mixture at a time and roll into balls. Place on cookie sheet and let dry uncovered 6 hours. Then put balls in freezer for 30 minutes. Melt bark and chips in microwave, stirring often. Remove balls from freezer and stab balls with a toothpick. Roll in the melted coating. Place on waxed paper to dry.

*   *   *

Beth and Rob retired near Atlanta to be near their son Myke and GRANDson, Dylan. We still get together at least once a year, even though we are a few states apart. We reminisce and laugh and explore new territory and laugh some more—just for the fun of it.

THE LAST DANCE

Me became We—that's the long and short of retirement. Fewer and fewer things put us on separate paths. Our individual identities have meshed leaving us to think alike and act alike. Even a stranger can match us up amid others in a large group. Scary. Countless times we have reminded each other of Grandma Smith who often said, "It's just you, me and the fence post." We've already lived alone together (ambiguity put aside) for twenty-five years. That's longer than the girls lived with us and longer than we lived with our families at home.

Ultimately, retirement indicates survival. Together, and sometimes in spite of each other, we conquered fears, anxieties, health issues, rearing children, career changes, lean times, busy times, fat times, obsessions, jealousies, enemies, natural disasters, loss of loved ones, new territory, tough decisions, and even Republican administrations.

We lived our whole life upsizing and now we downsize. We spent our younger years collecting and we're spending our older years giving away. In the final analysis, life is on the way up when we still have careers and on the way down once we retire. We're committed to enjoy the journey down as much as we did the journey going up. We don't have to worry anymore about where we're going or how we're going to get there. Been there, done that.

It's time to make right turns, only. Since the most treacherous part of driving is making left-hand turns, we turn right three times instead and end up exactly where we want to be without ever crossing the line of traffic. If we are going to survive the senior years, we need to make right turns. It's a foolproof rule. If we screw up, seven turns will get us back on track. This plan, which came from a great writer and humanitarian in Iowa, works best in the Corn State laid out in square miles. It's a little trickier in Texas Hill Country.

Sid began his retirement at sixty-two. Two years later, when I was fifty-nine, we started the last chapter of our lives together. We began by selling or donating anything that looked like work—lawn mowers, shovels, saws, and paintbrushes. We were through slaving with yard and housework. A friend suggested we were living the retirement that everyone dreams about. We found out that a lot of people couldn't or wouldn't do what we were about to do. But we weren't ones to dodge a risk.

With the house sold and all our remaining possessions, including cars, in storage, we put everything we thought we needed into four suitcases and boarded a plane headed to Guadalajara, Mexico. After four months in a little village in the mountains surrounding Lake Chapala, we were hooked on experiencing new cultures. We discovered that even strangers make great friends and that love and laughter are the essence of life anywhere. Everyone likes to party—fiesta, in this case.

Corn bread often graced the table whether we were in the homes of friends or at a native Mexican restaurant. Sid usually contributed his corn bread when the dinner was at our home. He has shared his recipe with lots of friends in Mexico and since returning to the states.

Sid's Corn Bread

1 1/2 cups flour

2/3 cup sugar

1/2 cup corn meal

1 T baking powder

1/2 tsp salt

1 1/4 cups milk

2 eggs lightly beaten

1/3 cup vegetable oil

3T melted butter

Preheat oven to 350. Combine liquid ingredients and mix well. Combine dry ingredients and add to liquid, stirring just until blended. Pour into greased 8 inch square pan. Bake 35 minutes or until toothpick comes out clean.

*   *   *

We were not anxious to leave Mexico but we did amid promises to return and friendships secured. The Midwest was familiar territory to celebrate the holidays with family and friends. They and we had survived our separation, and our storage-stuff was still happy to sit and wait out our next fling.

After a month, we took our four suitcases to Malta, smack dab in the middle of the Mediterranean. Again we stayed four months, dancing, sunning and listening to the music of the sea. And again, fun and laughter ruled. Socializing was even easier than in Mexico because everyone in Malta spoke English in addition to the native Maltese. The unique thing about the little island (the size of Des Moines) was the variety of European cultures that existed everywhere. A blink of the eye took us from Italy to Greece to France. The castles and temples, some 4000 years old, were amazing to us Iowans where most anything left standing after Progress swept through is less than a hundred years old.

A side trip to Tunisia provided what will probably be our only trip to the African continent and maybe our only trip to a Muslim country. A safari into the Sahara Desert ranks as our all-time favorite adventure.

We'll never forget a dozen or more food stands we passed where lunch was in various stages of preparations. The hanging lambs were either being stabbed, bled, or skinned. Some parts had already made it to the grills smoking heartily between the swinging carcasses and the tables filled with male diners dressed in black suits and ties. We had just passed the women and children working in the fields.

Finally, the time had come. We closed up our four suitcases and opened up some boxes out of storage. Our cars had slept for nearly a year, but they didn't complain when they had to get going again. We planted ourselves temporarily in an apartment in San Antonio to search for a permanent retirement location. Our post office box had served us well, but we needed a physical address if we wanted to vote for whatever candidate ran against Bush. Besides, a car license or a driver's license isn't available to nomads or the homeless, as we also called ourselves. Texas attracted us because of the weather, tax structure, cost of living and proximity to the Midwest and Mexico. We had explored Florida, Tennessee, Arkansas, and Arizona in the years leading up to retirement.

Besides making some wonderful new and lasting friends from our stay in Mexico, we enjoyed friends' visits from the states. Chris, Edie, and Sheila came to see for themselves what Mexico had to offer. Harold and Linda joined us for Thanksgiving. We ate turkey and dressing in swim cover-ups on the terrace. They all visited us in Texas and again gave their stamp of approval. Our friends didn't venture over to Malta.

It didn't take us long to find the place we wanted to call home for the retirement phase of our lives. We rationalized: the house was smaller than the last and we needed a new lawn mower, shovels, saws, and paint brushes anyway. We never looked back with regrets, but we do look forward to a lifetime of fun and adventure that awaits us.

We're blessed. We have our little house by the side of the road with lots of friends and family, near and far, so we can enjoy this journey. A few pots of flowers and an always-thirsty yard and garden provide a place to putter. Add three grandchildren and two daughters firmly entrenched in their own fulfilling lives. Turn on the music and dance to the love of life and each other. Throw a party, enjoy some fine dining, or grab a sandwich at a cowboy dive deep within the Hill Country. Play some golf or watch the ripples carry thoughts and dreams deeper into the lake. Take short trips, day trips, side trips and longed-for excursions.

My goal from years ago became our goal, and we, "just you, me, and the fence post", are living it.

Give me a house beside the Road
and let me be a Friend,
Give me a house beside the Lake
and let me reflect on the Water,
Give me a house beside the Woods
and let me commune with Nature,
Give me a house beside the Garden
and let me share beauty with Flowers.

Long before retirement, we learned that life is not always a party, but we might as well dance. When given the choice to sit out or dance, we danced. We started out dancing. We should go out dancing. Robert Frost wrote in *Swinger of Birches*, "That would be good both going and coming back."

AFTERWORD

Writing down my memories has been pure enjoyment. As I thought back over events in my life and recalled the special people who played an important role, I gained insight and pleasure that had escaped me all those busy years.

From my perspective, I did what I set out to do. I shared my memories. I shared a few pieces of myself so my GRANDkids would have a part of me to keep. Carter, Olivia, and Nolan are my treasures, and I hope in some small way my life experiences will help enrich each of their life stories.

It wasn't always easy to reveal my thoughts. Sometimes I dug really deep and discovered things I hadn't allowed myself to think about before. Just the computer and me, we sat for hours. Sometimes I cried and sometimes I laughed. Sometimes the writing was easy and other times it was pretty painful.

In the beginning I anticipated telling my story of survival. By the end I had learned that I was the lucky beneficiary of life-changing experiences. Many loving people had helped me develop the upbeat side of life. Collectively, they taught me to dance.

Regretfully, several classmates, friends and relatives who are embedded in my mind have passed. Still others are no longer in the relationships and circumstances referenced in my story. Many names have changed due to marriage and shedding of nicknames. Hopefully I didn't offend anyone by my conscious decision to identify and position people in the past as I recalled it.

I was nearly finished with my reminiscing when the title came to me. And no sooner did I have a title, than I thought it necessitated the addition of favorite recipes. I wrestled with the idea and decided, after some encouragement from May and Janice, to include those that had been requested the most over the years. By the time I had sifted thoughtfully through my collection, I realized that recipes are truly part of my legacy and that the GRANDkids should know their origins. The recipes were added.

Those who have known me awhile probably didn't learn anything new. I have told parts of my story a zillion times. Probably every tale has been woven at least once for some willing listener. I can see a few readers shaking their heads. That could be a good thing or it could be a bad thing, as Missy Chrissy would say.

Most of all, you heard **my** voice. I didn't write with any concern for what authors or editors might expect. I broke every rule of composition I taught to students. I took liberties with traditional grammar, punctuation, and spelling. I didn't even red pencil my own work, leaving mistakes right where I had put them. I simply wrote from my heart.

Hopefully, I honored family and friends, but even more importantly, I trust I didn't hurt anyone. That was never my intention because I've learned along the way that sometimes truth hurts. In the end, I didn't tell EVERYTHING. I didn't tell the whole truth because I didn't want to be hurtful. More than once I applied my grandmother's adage, "When in doubt, don't." I had to serve as my own censor on this do-it-yourself project.

AFTERWORD

Some friends and family who knew I was writing my memoirs were quite curious and others couldn't have cared less. A few wanted a sneak peak. Beth wanted someone she trusted to pre-read the manuscript. Friends grew tired of hearing about the project and wondered if I would ever deliver the goods.

Sid is the hero. He never read a word, never asked what I was writing, and never offered any comments, although he certainly would have been entitled to lobby on behalf of himself. He gave me the time and space I needed to sort through my feelings plus encouragement galore to get them down on paper.

My project was more fun and less tedious because Sid eagerly did some of the research for me. When I couldn't come up with a name or when I wanted to be sure my facts were straight, he would dig through the stored keepsakes or search the Internet for confirmation. He always produced his reports without comments or questions regarding how or why I was using the information.

Thanks to Dave for designing the cover. It's an awesome task trying to make your mother-in-law look good. A thank-you is probably all he'll get for his efforts, but I already gave him my daughter. That's a lot for any mother to do.

Dave asked for a childhood picture to use in his cover design. I chose one that was taken shortly after my leg cast was removed following the accident. Uncle Bill dressed me up, brushed my hair without quite getting the part in the middle of my head, and took me to Hayford's Drug Store for the photo shoot. The bracelet spelling out MERRY is on my left arm.

It's May of 2007, and I'm finished writing. I have a bunch more living to do with cherished friends and family. Fun lurks just around the corner. If all goes well and the sun continues to shine, I can make scads more memories, but I don't plan to make any more books.

to Nolan, Carter, and Olivia

I hope you dance.

XXX and OOO from Grandma Merry

978-0-595-45248-4
0-595-45248-5